FISH

FISH

Recipes and Techniques for Freshwater Fish

JON WIPFLI

HARVARD COMMON PRESS

Brimming with creative inspiration, how-to projects, and useful information to enrich your everyday life, Quarto Knows is a favorite destination for those pursuing their interests and passions. Visit our site and dig deeper with our books into your area of interest: Quarto Creates, Quarto Cooks, Quarto Homes, Quarto Lives, Quarto Drives, Quarto Explores, Quarto Gifts, or Quarto Kids.

© 2019 Quarto Publishing Group USA Inc.
Text © 2019 Jon Wipfli

First Published in 2019 by The Harvard Common Press, an imprint of The Quarto Group,
100 Cummings Center, Suite 265-D,
Beverly, MA 01915, USA.
T (978) 282-9590 F (978) 283-2742
QuartoKnows.com

The Harvard Common Press titles are also available at discount for retail, wholesale, promotional, and bulk purchase. For details, contact the Special Sales Manager by email at specialsales@quarto.com or by mail at The Quarto Group, Attn: Special Sales Manager, 100 Cummings Center, Suite 265-D, Beverly, MA 01915, USA.

23 22 21 20 19   1 2 3 4 5

ISBN: 978-0-7603-6407-9

Digital edition published in 2019

Library of Congress Cataloging-in-Publication Data available

Names: Wipfli, Jon, author.

Title: Fish : the lake-to-kitchen cookbook / Jon Wipfli.

Description: Beverly, MA : The Harvard Common Press, 2019. | Includes index.

Identifiers: LCCN 2019006967 | ISBN 9780760364079 (paper over board)

Subjects: LCSH: Cooking (Fish) | LCGFT: Cookbooks.

Classification: LCC TX747 .W57 2019 | DDC 641.3/92--dc23 LC record available at https://lccn.loc.gov/2019006967

Design: Amy Sly
Cover Image: Colleen Eversman
Page Layout: Amy Sly
Photography: Colleen Eversman

Printed in China

CONTENTS

CRAPPIE, BLUEGILL
& PERCH

CATFISH, STURGEON,
MUSKIE & WHITEFISH

CRAWDADS

INTRODUCTION

In this book, I cover multiple species of fish, ranging everywhere from bluegill to muskie, but could not reasonably cover every species of landlocked fish. For the purpose of functionality I cover the species of which I have witnessed the most consumption. There is a plethora of species I would have liked to cover and, with any luck, those species will be covered in a future book.

My goal in writing this book was to create recipes that can be made by chefs of any level while incorporating various techniques and ingredients that may be unfamiliar to some. Beyond that, I hope it creates an increased interest in obtaining your own protein and getting outdoors and fishing! I would love to hear from readers about what should be included in future editions!

I hope this book is helpful to you. If you have questions about the book or need help navigating a recipe, please reach out to Jon.Wipfli@gmail.com or find me on Instagram @theminnesotaspoon and I'll do my best to help.

PART 1
FISHING

To research and write this book, I had to do quite a bit of fishing. This went far beyond solo trips. I was lucky enough to connect with some incredible fishermen and learn new fishing techniques along the way. We fished for steelhead and whitefish in Michigan, lake trout on Lake Superior, muskie and walleye in Wisconsin, and made it to the Dakotas for some ice fishing. It was eye-opening to see how different people specialize in one style of fishing—and the work, time, and money they put into it.

To people who do this daily, it seems like simple work, but for an outsider looking in, it's outstanding. The knowledge I took away from these fishermen on fish habitat, habits, and cycles was astounding. For example, I watched an expert fisherman navigate the endless waters of Lake Superior knowing exactly where specific lake-bottom terrains appeared and observed another knowing exactly which night the herring run would occur based on when the snow melts. This is knowledge gained slowly over years of persistence mixed with trial and error, all while typically not being able to see the subject until it breaks the plane of the water. There's an underappreciated wealth of knowledge these individuals carry, and I have an immense respect for them.

I grew up fishing the waters of northern Wisconsin, never taking it too seriously. As a kid and young adult, my friends, family, and I would often catch walleye, gill, crappie, bass, and northern pike and walleye pike near our family cabin. In my twenties I moved to Montana and found an immense amount of pleasure in learning to fly-fish its massive rivers and the beautiful lakes I found nestled high in the mountains. In my late twenties I caught the muskie bug after my close circle of hunting friends introduced me to the sport. Again, I was lucky enough to spend time in boats with folks more knowledgeable than I, chasing monster muskies and occasionally hook into one myself.

The more time we spent in boats not catching muskies (so, about 98 percent of the time), the more I learned that success when fishing isn't measured by fish caught, follows, or inches measured. It's all about getting outside, drinking some beers with friends, and learning about what's happening in the natural world that surrounds us. No matter your skill level, there's an easy way to get out and sink a line into the water, and I can't think of a better way to spend a day.

BIG PICTURE

Beyond the sporting aspect of it, lake and river fishing is generally a sustainable and affordable way to obtain food. Fish management and stocking, for the most part, is well regulated and well done. Dollars spent for fishing licenses provide countless jobs and help protect our right to use these lands. Personally, it's the best money I spend every year. If you enjoy the privilege of being able to use public lands as much as I do, continue to buy those licenses, bring your friends out on adventures, and find other ways to support public lands.

All this said, this book is a cookbook, not a fishing book. I am not a fish biologist nor an expert fisherman. Fishing is an activity in which I've found meaning and pleasure over the course of my life, but I am in no way an expert resource on the subject. My specialty lies in cooking, and I find it very satisfying, on many levels, to expertly prepare food I've killed. As always, be mindful of what you take and how you take it. **Always follow all applicable laws and regulations.** And, if possible, find out what condition the lake is in and if it has a healthy and robust fish population.

NOTE

It's also good to keep in mind that eating any large predatory fish comes with some health risks, mostly stemming from mercury content and other containments in the waters. They should not be eaten in large quantities or fed to children, pregnant women, or the elderly. If you do decide to catch and keep one, please do due diligence on the fish, the fishing habitat, and any and all health risks associated with it.

EATING

Wild game cookbooks can be challenging to organize because more than one fish or piece of game can work for many recipes. Generally speaking, I think people with a freezer full of fish will look for some flavor combinations that interest them and go with whatever's just been caught (or is in the freezer). For example, you can substitute perch for crappie in the Crappie Escabeche (page 107) without any real effect on the quality of the dish—and you can find examples like that across the entire book. Grouping recipes into substitutable categories of fish reflects that formatting. Fish that I believe can be easily substituted for another find their way into the same groups, so feel free to substitute within those categories with minimal risk to the end results. But even that is not a hard rule, as you can move different species around to various recipes throughout the book once you learn the different characteristics of the fish.

I approached this book in a similar fashion to the way I approached my first book, *Venison*. I include a mix of more elevated dishes that require a bit of technique, as well as meals that can be easily cooked over a fire (and just as easily enjoyed). I try to strip my recipes of extra steps to keep the majority accessible to cooks of all skill levels.

I also think of these recipes as a baseline for a final dish. Recipes and ingredients have countless variables, making it difficult to re-create a dish exactly as written under the best of circumstances. I recommend taking ownership of these recipes and playing with them to suit your tastes. Using the techniques and the base recipes will get you off to a great start. However, using your own tastes to alternate spices, vegetables, seasonings—even swapping out the fish for another type—will be a delicious exploration.

With any luck, you'll soon be sharing these recipes with the same family members and friends you were with when you caught that fish. Good luck on the lake and have fun in the kitchen!

FIRES

Cooking over live fire imparts flavors to any meal that you can't manufacture any other way. Live fire is one of my favorite ways to cook and is mentioned frequently in this book, so I want to review the basics of a good fire.

Whether it's a grill, an open pit, or any other grilling unit, here are some tips for open-flame cooking—mostly based on using charcoal and wood.

For a **high-temperature grill**, I like to use natural lump charcoal mixed with small chunks of hardwood, preferably oak. With this method it's best to get the lump charcoal hot and add the chunks of wood to get them smoking. Once they're black and smoldering, it is a good time to add the protein to the grill.

When operating with **straight hardwood only,** I like to get a good base of wood coals going from burning logs at a high temperature and then add a log or two on top to get a nice smoky flavor. It's unrealistic to judge a certain surface temperature, but a grill anywhere in the 400°F to 650°F (200°C to 343°C) range is suitable for most applications.

When I write "start a fire," this is what I'm referring to.

Depending on the heat of the grill you may have to rotate and flip your fish less or more often.

For optimum results make sure your grill and grates are clean.

To prevent sticking, coat the grates with a light layer of grapeseed oil and make sure they're hot before adding the fish.

Practice cooking over open fires. It's an imperfect art but has lots of benefits. Finding a rhythm over the fire will develop over time, and your success rates will be nearly perfect.

PART 2

FISH

CLEANING & FILLETING

Fish species vary widely in taste and texture. Fish can have a sweet, lighter flavor, such as walleye, or a heavier, oilier flavor as seen in salmon. Some have a lighter and flakier texture, such as bluegill, compared to the steak-like quality of sturgeon. Preferring one quality another is up to the consumer, but, with few exceptions, all these fish are better eaten when as fresh as possible.

If you're purchasing fish from a fishmonger, look for these signs to ensure you are getting the freshest fish possible.

The eyes should be bright, not clouded.

The flesh should bounce back when poked and it should not be mushy.

The fish should smell fresh. All fish have a "fishy" smell, but it should be a clean fish scent.

Trust your gut. If something seems amiss, it very easily could be. Don't buy that fish.

Before cooking, or even butchering, fish, there are two crucial steps to finalize your catch: proper cleaning and proper storage. These are both simple steps but take some diligence to do correctly. After you pull your catch out of the water, gut it as soon as possible and put the fish on ice. Keep the fish on ice up until the time you clean it and immediately put it back on ice until you cook or freeze it. While in culinary school, a professor used to tell me if you start a recipe with crap, you'll end up with crap. If the fish isn't properly cleaned and stored, you'll find yourself in that pickle.

CLEANING

Fresh fish are susceptible to quick muscle breakdown and turning into something you don't want to eat. Gutting and cleaning fish quickly for preparation or the freezer is crucial to getting the best possible product. Killing, gutting, cleaning, scaling, and cooling the fish rapidly yield the best results. I can be a bit over the top when I clean fish—removing the guts and scales before removing the fillets. The other way I approach it is skipping both of those steps (ignoring the gutting process) and just removing the fillets. When you're not cooking a whole fish or cooking skin-on fish, it's much quicker to skip scaling, but I do appreciate having scales off the skin while removing the meat from the skin. Take the process to your level of needs.

Always use a sharp knife (I like to use either a flexible boning knife or hard Japanese steel) and have a large, clean cutting board available and a sink nearby.

SCALING

Scaling comes first if you're planning to cook the fish immediately or freeze the fish with the scales off. When scaling fish, cleanup is easier if you have a fine drain catch in your sink. I find the process much simpler if the fish is cold, somewhere around refrigerator temperature (34°F, or 1°C).

In my experience, I like to scale fish before freezing so that I know all the frozen fish are consistently prepped. If a label wears out or I can't identify whether the fish is scaled through the packaging, I know what I'm getting before the fish is thawed.

Scaling the fish for fresh cooking is also a great option. The skin of fish is one of the most flavorful parts of the animal; it helps keep in moisture while cooking and eliminates the risk of meat loss during the butchering process.

To scale a fish effectively, you'll need a couple things:

Scaler: A great scaler can easily be found online for less than $20. It will save you a boatload of time and last forever, so it's money well spent.

Running water: Whether a stream or a faucet, water helps keep your workstation clean and ready to butcher.

STEPS FOR SCALING FISH

1. If desired, remove all the fins of the fish with a pair of kitchen shears.

2. Under running water, run your fish scaler against the grain of the fish until all the scales are removed **(A)**.

3. It's common to have some scales left near the fin areas of the fish and on the underbelly. Double-check those areas to make sure all scales are removed.

A

GUTTING

The first step to gutting a pile of fish is cracking a cold one. After that it's pretty easy. Cut shallowly from the anus to the gills and pull out all the smelly stuff. If you do have a pile of fish, gut them all at once and then move on to butchery to help avoid cross contamination. Once all the guts are out, give the fish an extra rinse to make sure all the particulates are out as well.

STEPS FOR GUTTING FISH

1. Place a sharp knife into the anus of the fish, just barely through the flesh **(A)**.

2. Cutting as close to the skin as possible, cut the fish up toward the beginning of the gills **(B)**.

3. With kitchen shears, snip anything connecting the guts to the fish from inside the throat cavity. Remove anything in the cavity by pulling it out with your hands **(C)** and rinse the inside of the fish thoroughly **(D)**.

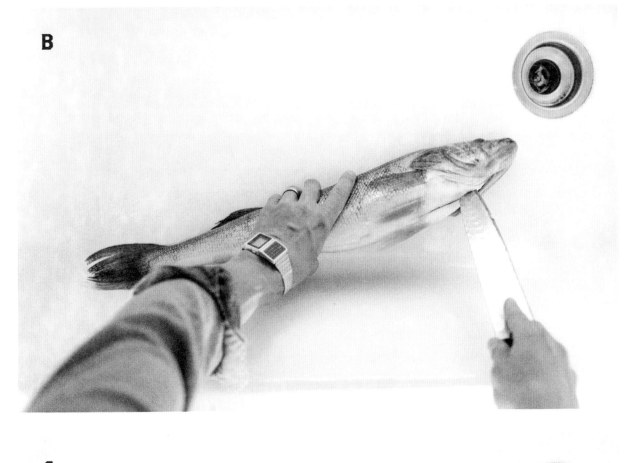

D

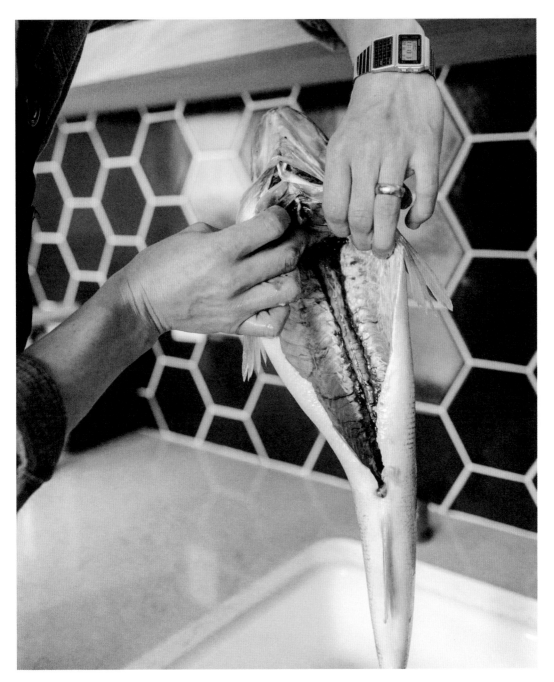

A clean cavity should look about like this.

Once the fish is gutted, it's time to either scale it, store it for future cooking, or cook it immediately. If you're not scaling before freezing, skip to page 35 and then come back to scaling (see page 28).

STORING

Proper storage is crucial for fish. It makes all the difference between enjoying your catch and ruining it before it ever hits the kitchen. Fortunately, there are multiple ways you can store fish to keep it tasting its best.

When I store fresh fish in a restaurant, I place the fish on top of a stainless steel perforated pan inserted into a deeper stainless steel pan. I cover the fish tightly with plastic wrap and place a bag of ice on top of the fish in the refrigerator. While it may seem like a bit much, this technique is the best way to store fresh fish and give it the longest shelf life. If you don't want to go through that process of fresh fish storage, I recommend storing fish in a container that gives it the ability to lose moisture but not sit in its own juices. Any sort of perforated pan placed over a container to catch drippings will do.

If you're planning to freeze the fish, best success is with vacuum sealing whole, gutted, scaled fish. Keeping the fish whole means less surface area is exposed, which helps retain moisture in the fish. Freezing fish in blocks of ice is a good technique as well, but I prefer the space and time efficiency of using a vacuum sealer. Freezing in tightly sealed resealable bags is also a good solution, but freezer burn will creep up on you much quicker, so plan to eat it sooner rather than later.

FILLETING

Congratulations, you now have a fish that's ready to butcher! This brings me to my friend Anderson, who volunteered his butchering skills in service of this book. Anderson works with fish of all varieties at a fish company called The Fish Guys located in Minneapolis, Minnesota. The sheer volume of fish he sees and works with makes him a great resource for all things that live in the water. When we came up short catching fish for this book, Anderson and The Fish Guys were right there with something to fill in the spot.

There are two types of fish filleting for the fish used in this book. First is for your standard-issue walleye, bluegill, perch, and so on, and second is for northern and muskie. There are minor differences in all the fish, but the basics are the same. With northerns and muskies you have to look out for Y bones, which are fine bones that stand up through the midsection of the fish; the rest can be butchered without this in mind. For the purposes of this book I refer to the cleaning of northern and muskie as a "five fillet" fish. The more traditional method, I'll call the "two fillet" method.

I've seen a few overarching techniques for filleting fish, but my favorite comes from Anderson, who can move through a pile of fish damn quickly. Starting with a gutted fish he simply cuts in front of the gills and then straight across the backbone, keeping the rib bones in place on the fillet. He then flips the fillet, removes the ribs, and fillets the fish cleanly.

The following steps assume you are working with gutted fish. If you plan to keep the skin on for cooking, scale the fish before taking fillets off the body.

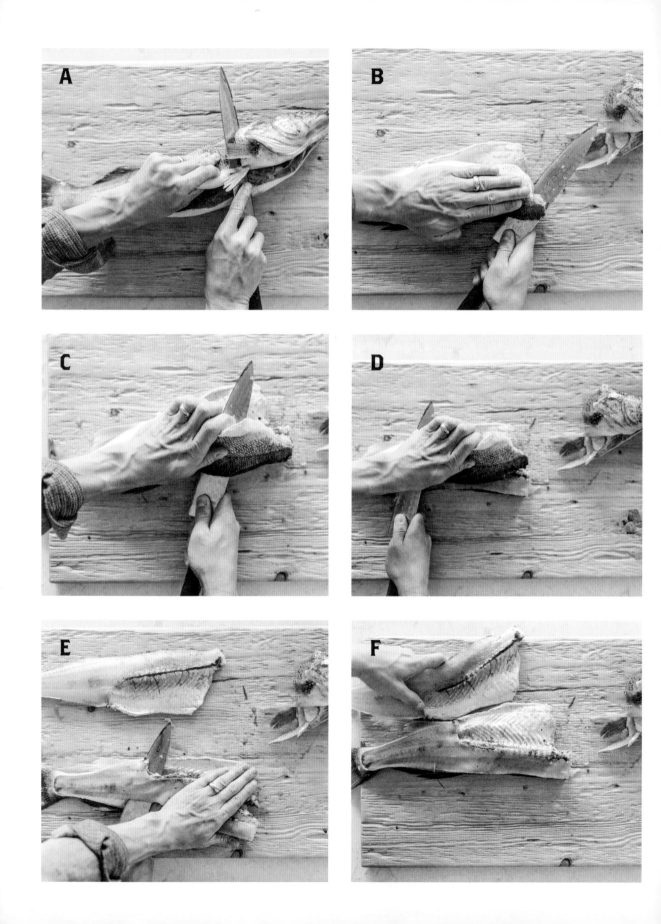

FILLETING "TWO FILLET" FISH

1. Place your sharp knife just in back of the gills of the fish **(A)**.

2. Cut down toward the spine until your blade hits the spine. Cut through the spine and remove the head and set aside.

3. Place your knife blade parallel to the spine at the opening where the head was **(B)**.

4. Making sure your knife is running underneath the open gut side of the meat, run your knife along the spine of the fish all the way through the base of the tail and remove the fillet **(C & D)**.

5. Place your knife parallel on the other side of the spine and run your knife down the spine to remove it from the flesh **(E & F)**.

6. With the flesh facing upward, carefully remove the ribs by running your knife under the rib cage **(G & H)**.

   If keeping the skin on, skip steps 7 and 8.

7. Run your knife between the flesh and the skin at the tail end of the fish for about 1 inch (2.5 cm). Make a small incision with your knife into the skin of the fish by the tip of the tail, large enough to poke your finger into.

8. With your finger anchoring the skin of the fish, run your knife, angled toward the skin, down the rest of the fillet.

9. Remove pin bones toward the front of the fish by cutting around the line where you can feel them or remove them with bone tweezers.

You should now have a boneless, skinless fillet ready to cook and eat! Use any trim for Basic Fish Stock (page 151). If you want to leave the skin on, remove scales before butchery and skip steps 7 and 8.

FILLETING NORTHERNS AND MUSKIES ("FIVE FILLET" FISH)

1. Place your gutted and scaled fish on a cutting board, stomach side down.

2. Place a knife behind the head at the back of the gill plate and cut it down to right above the spine. Run the knife just across the top of the spine all the way down to the tail and remove the back fillet. Set aside.

3. Place the fish on its side.

4. About three-fourths of the way down the fish toward the tail, run your knife down to the spine.

5. Turn your knife to align with the spine and remove the tail fillet. Repeat on the other side.

6. Place the fish back on its stomach.

7. Look down into the meat and locate the Y bones.

8. Cut along the outside of the bones down toward the cutting board and remove the fillet around the ribs. Repeat on the other side.

9. If desired, remove the meat from the skin using the aforementioned filleting technique.

10. Use all scraps for Basic Fish Stock (page 151).

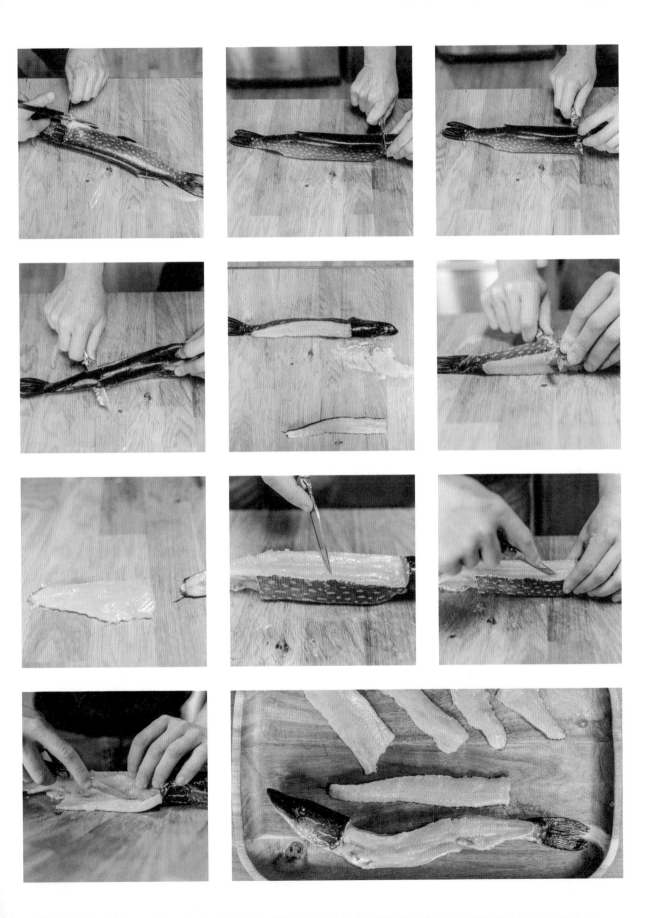

PART 3

RECIPES

SALMON & TROUT

RECIPES

WOOD-FIRED SALMON

Salmon definitely is best when it's as fresh as possible. This recipe doesn't require many steps or ingredients, so any signs of deteriorating fish will be noticeable in the finished dish. The simple combination of super fresh fish, lemon, salt, and smoke is perfect. I originally made this as an appetizer to pick at right off the hot griddle. Turn to Wood-Fired Salmon with Fennel Salad and Seasoned Yogurt (page 49) for a more complete recipe fit for plating. These steaks could also be used elsewhere, like in the Catfish Tacos with Crema and Tomatillo Salsa (page 119). Use any leftovers for a salmon quiche (see Steelhead Trout Quiche with Fiddleheads and Arugula, page 66) or pudgy pie (see Smoked Trout–Stuffed Pudgy Pie Hash Browns (page 62)!

YIELD: Serves 4 to 6

INGREDIENTS

Grapeseed oil, for cooking

1 bunch fresh flat-leaf parsley

1 lemon, sliced (save the ends for squeezing)

Four 8-ounce (225 g) salmon fillets

Kosher salt

PROCEDURE

Start a fire in your grill with natural lump charcoal (see page 23). Once the coals are hot and roasting, add a log or two of your chosen wood (hickory or apple). Let the logs burn down until the flames subside. You want a temperature around 450°F (230°C).

Drizzle a large cast-iron skillet with grapeseed oil. Spread the parsley evenly over the pan. Place the lemon slices on top of the parsley. Top the lemon with the salmon fillets. Lightly coat the salmon with grapeseed oil and season with salt.

Place the skillet on the grill grate and close the grill lid. Slightly crack the grill vents. Smoke should be able to escape, but the grill should also hold a bit of smoke. Cook for 6 to 7 minutes, depending on your grill's temperature, or until the fish reaches an internal temperature of 145°F (63°C) measured with an instant-read thermometer.

Squeeze some lemon from the reserved ends over the top and pick away, or transfer to plates and serve.

FENNEL SALAD
with Wood-Fired Salmon and Seasoned Yogurt

This recipe pairs the Wood-Fired Salmon (page 48) with a rich, herbaceous yogurt and crispy fennel salad. Fennel has a strong licorice flavor that pairs well with fish, and cutting it thinly on a mandolin makes the taste a little less overwhelming. The final product is light and crisp, leaving you refreshed!

YIELD: Serves 4 to 6

INGREDIENTS FOR THE SEASONED YOGURT

1 cup (230 g) plain full-fat Greek yogurt

1 tablespoon (6 g) fennel seed

1 tablespoon (20 g) honey

1 teaspoon kosher salt

1 teaspoon freshly cracked black pepper

INGREDIENTS FOR THE FENNEL SALAD AND SALMON

1 garlic clove, thinly sliced

1 Thai chile, thinly sliced

1 small shallot, minced

2 tablespoons (30 ml) champagne vinegar or freshly squeezed lemon juice

2 fennel bulbs, quartered, cored, and sliced as thinly as possible (see tip)

Kosher salt

6 tablespoons (90 ml) grapeseed oil

¼ cup (16 g) fresh parsley, roughly chopped

1 recipe Wood-Fired Salmon (page 48)

PROCEDURE

To make the seasoned yogurt: In a small bowl, whisk all the ingredients for the seasoned yogurt. Cover and refrigerate until needed.

To make the fennel salad and salmon: In a large bowl, stir together the garlic, Thai chile, shallot, and vinegar. Let sit for about 30 minutes.

Add the sliced fennel to the vinegar mixture. Season to taste with salt and toss to combine. Let the mixture sit for 10 minutes to soften the fennel. Add the grapeseed oil and parsley and toss to combine.

To plate, place a spoonful of yogurt on the plate, a salmon fillet on top, and finish with a bit of fennel salad.

COOKING TIP

A mandolin is a slicing device that will change your life in the kitchen! It will help you cut things extremely evenly and thinly in a fraction of the time it takes with a knife. Watch your fingertips, though, and use a thick glove to protect your slicing hand. Cutting your finger on a mandolin is a mistake you'll make only once.

SALT, SUGAR, AND DILL-CURED SALMON

Curing with salt, sugar, and dill is one of the most traditional methods for making cured salmon. It's a tried-and-true technique you can't go wrong with *as long as you use fresh salmon*. In the recipe following (page 52), I pair this salmon with crème fraîche and some traditional accents on toast—but I encourage you to use your imagination. It can make its way into omelets, top bagels or eggs Benedict, or be plainly sliced onto a charcuterie platter. It's an extremely versatile ingredient. You can also use this same process with other fish, such as trout or bass.

YIELD: Serves 10 to 12 when used as part of other recipes

INGREDIENTS

1 cup (300 g) kosher salt

1 cup (200 g) sugar

Two 24-ounce (680 g) salmon fillets, bones removed as needed

2 bunches fresh dill, roughly chopped

PROCEDURE

In a small bowl, stir together the salt and sugar until blended. Sprinkle the bottom of an 8 x 12-inch (20 x 30 cm) glass baking dish with a layer of the salt and sugar mixture and a layer of dill. Lightly season the skin side of one salmon fillet with the salt and sugar mixture and place it, skin side down, in the baking dish. Aggressively season the flesh side of that fillet with the salt and sugar mixture and spread a handful of dill over the fish.

Aggressively season the flesh side of the second fillet and place it on top of the fillet in the dish so that flesh is resting on flesh. Aggressively season the skin side of the exposed salmon and spread the remaining dill over the top.

Cover the salmon with plastic wrap and place some weights, such as bricks or a couple of large tomato cans resting on a sheet of parchment, on it, pressing the salmon down evenly. Refrigerate. Flip the fish every 12 hours and drain the juices collected each time it's flipped. Do this four times over a curing period of 48 hours.

After 48 hours, wipe away any excess salt with a damp cloth and the salmon is ready to eat. When you're ready to serve it, remove the skin.

CURED SALMON
with Crème Fraîche, Lemon, and Dill on Toast

This is a straightforward dish that seems to please everyone. The star is diced cured salmon with some added fat in the form of crème fraîche, fresh lemon for acidity, and dill for a pop of freshness. Shallots and capers add to the depth of flavor, but aren't necessary for a great-tasting end result. If you don't have time to cure the salmon yourself, buy cured salmon for this recipe.

YIELD: Serves 4 to 6 as a snack

INGREDIENTS

½ cup (112 g) crème fraîche

1 tablespoon (9 g) capers, rinsed and chopped

Kosher salt

Freshly ground black pepper

4 to 6 slices hearty bread, such as rye, toasted

1 pound (454 g) Salt, Sugar, and Dill–Cured Salmon (page 51), thinly sliced

½ cup (70 g) Quick Cucumber Pickles (page 108)

½ cup (80 g) Pickled Red Onion, drained of liquid (page 127)

2 teaspoons freshly squeezed lemon juice

1 tablespoon (4 g) fresh dill

PROCEDURE

In a small bowl, stir together the crème fraîche and capers. Season the mixture with a pinch of salt and pepper. Lightly spread the toast with the crème fraîche. Fold slices of salmon onto the coated bread. Top with quick pickles and red onion. Sprinkle a bit of fresh lemon juice over the fish and garnish with dill.

DEVILED EGGS
with Smoked Salmon

I feel like everyone has experienced a few versions of deviled eggs. When done well, the filling should be bright, fresh, and creamy. The eggs should have good texture from being perfectly cooked (see tip), and the toppings should add the final send-off to deviled egg heaven.

This is my standard deviled egg recipe, but topped with a bit of smoked salmon. If you have cured salmon, salmon roe, caviar, or pretty much anything else sitting around the house, it can be used as a substitute for the wood-fired salmon. Perfecting the filling is all about using homemade aioli. If you want the perfect eggs, take your time!

YIELD: Serves 4 to 6 as a snack

INGREDIENTS

12 large hard-boiled eggs, shelled

⅓ cup (75 g) Homemade Aioli (page 87), plus more as needed

2 tablespoons (30 g) stone-ground mustard

2 teaspoons garam masala

1 teaspoon freshly squeezed lemon juice, plus more to taste

1 teaspoon Tabasco

6 ounces (170 g) Wood-Fired Salmon (page 48; leftovers work well)

Kosher salt

Freshly ground black pepper

Paprika, for garnishing

Fresh dill sprigs, for garnishing

PROCEDURE

Halve the eggs lengthwise. Remove the yolks from the whites and set the whites aside. Press the yolks through a tamis or fine-mesh strainer, or put them through a potato ricer, so they fall in fine particles.

In a large bowl, stir together the aioli, mustard, garam masala, lemon juice, and Tabasco. Using a rubber spatula gently fold the egg yolks into the aioli. Taste and add more lemon juice, salt, and pepper, as needed. You can also add more aioli if you want a creamier consistency.

Transfer the egg and aioli mixture into a piping bag with a medium tip. Pipe the filling into the egg whites. Alternatively, spoon them into the egg cavities. Top with the salmon, a sprinkle of paprika, and a dill sprig.

COOKING TIP

If you're having trouble making well-cooked eggs, combine the eggs and water in a saucepan and bring to a boil over high heat. Remove the pan from the heat and place a lid on the pan. Let the eggs sit for 7 minutes. Add ice to the water and let your eggs cool before peeling.

WILD RICE–STUFFED STEELHEAD TROUT

with Asparagus Salad and Beurre Blanc

I first learned of this recipe while fishing for steelhead trout in Michigan's Upper Peninsula. The pairing of two celebrated Midwest ingredients makes for a great flavor combination, and the wild rice adds a nice bite of texture. Beurre blanc (a French butter sauce) ties the whole thing together and adds the perfect amount of savory to the dish. Make sure the wild rice is fully cooked before stuffing the trout, as it won't continue to cook in the fish.

YIELD: Serves 6 to 8

INGREDIENTS FOR THE WILD RICE

2 tablespoons (28 g) unsalted butter

3 celery stalks, diced

1 medium carrot, diced

1 medium yellow onion, diced

2 garlic cloves, thinly sliced

1 tablespoon (3 g) minced fresh thyme leaves

8 ounces (225 g) wild rice

1 quart (960 ml) chicken stock, plus more as needed

Kosher salt

INGREDIENTS FOR THE ASPARAGUS SALAD

8 large asparagus stalks

1 teaspoon freshly squeezed lemon juice

1 tablespoon (15 ml) grapeseed oil

Kosher salt

PROCEDURE

To make the wild rice: In a 6- to 8-quart (5.8 to 7.6 L) pot over medium heat, melt the butter. Add the celery, carrot, onion, garlic, and thyme. Sweat the ingredients until soft, about 4 minutes.

Add the wild rice. Toast for 1 to 2 minutes, stirring. Add the chicken stock and bring the mixture to a simmer. Simmer until the wild rice has popped and is fully cooked, about 50 minutes. Add more chicken stock as needed, if the rice gets dry. Taste and season with salt. Let cool at room temperature.

While the rice cooks, make the asparagus salad: Using a mandolin or vegetable peeler, thinly shave the asparagus lengthwise. In a medium bowl, combine the shaved asparagus, lemon juice, and grapeseed oil. Toss to coat. Taste and season with salt. Set aside.

To make the steelhead trout: Preheat the oven to 425°F (220°C). Lightly coat a sheet pan with grapeseed oil and set aside. Open the cavity of the fish and fill it with as much of the cooked wild rice as possible. (You'll probably have some rice left over that you can warm and serve on the side.) Using butcher's twine, tie the fish as closed as possible without squeezing out all the wild rice. Season the outside of the fish with salt and pepper.

Place the fish on the prepared sheet pan. Bake for 45 to 50 minutes, or until the fish reaches 145°F (63°C) measured with an instant-read thermometer and is cooked to your liking.

recipe continues

INGREDIENTS FOR THE STEELHEAD TROUT

Grapeseed oil, for coating the sheet pan

One 3- to 4-pound (1.35 to 1.8 kg) steelhead trout, gutted and scaled

Kosher salt

Freshly ground black pepper

INGREDIENTS FOR BEURRE BLANC

1 medium shallot, finely diced

3 tablespoons (45 ml) white wine vinegar

1 tablespoon (9 g) peppercorns

1 tablespoon (5 g) coriander seeds

8 tablespoons (1 stick, or 112 g) cold unsalted butter, cubed

Splash heavy cream

Freshly squeezed lemon juice, for seasoning

Kosher salt

If you enjoy eating the skin, turn on the broiler. Place the fish under the boiler for 1 to 2 minutes to crisp the skin a bit. Remove the fish from the oven and let cool for 10 minutes before serving.

While the fish cooks, make the beurre blanc: In a 2-quart (960 ml) saucepan over medium heat, combine the shallot, vinegar, peppercorns, and coriander. Bring to a simmer. Cook until the liquid reduces to the consistency of a glaze, about 6 minutes.

Strain the liquid through a fine-mesh strainer into a small heatproof bowl. Return the liquid to the pan and place it over very low heat. One at a time, add the butter cubes, whisking constantly until each melts into the liquid before adding the next. Work slowly so the butter doesn't separate. Once all the butter is incorporated, whisk in the heavy cream. Season to taste with lemon juice and salt.

To serve: Cut the twine away from the fish. Pull off some of the meat and plate with a scoop of wild rice from the cavity. Ladle on the beurre blanc and garnish with a handful of asparagus salad.

LAKE TROUT IN FOIL
with Fennel, Mushrooms, and Sugar-Cured Jalapeños

Cooking over open flames and in aluminum foil is second nature to me. When I began studying French cuisine, the technique and ingredients were elevated and given a name that sounded new and exciting to me—*en papillote*, which means "in paper." It's the same idea here, but with foil instead.

The benefit of cooking in paper or foil is all the moisture stays within the cooking vessel, producing an extra-succulent dish. There's also something to the less-than-precise nature of the process that seems to make the food taste even better. Bonus: there are no dishes to worry about cleaning if you and your guests are good with eating straight from the foil! Arugula salad (see Sturgeon and Roast Beets with Yogurt, Grapefruit, and Arugula Salad, page 131) makes a great optional garnish.

The sugar-cured jalapeños take 24 hours to prepare, so you will need to plan ahead. If jalapeños are too hot for your palate, use bell peppers or a mix of peppers for a milder garnish.

YIELD: Serves 6 to 8

INGREDIENTS FOR THE SUGAR-CURED JALAPEÑOS

8 jalapeño peppers, thinly sliced

1 cup (200 g) sugar

INGREDIENTS FOR THE LAKE TROUT IN FOIL

1 pound (454 g) button mushrooms, cleaned and halved

1 fennel bulb, cleaned and diced

1 tablespoon (15 ml) melted unsalted butter

1 tablespoon (3 g) fresh thyme leaves

Kosher salt

1 lemon, sliced

One 3- to 4-pound (1.35 to 1.8 kg) lake trout, filleted and boned

PROCEDURE

To make the sugar-cured jalapeños: In a medium bowl, toss together the jalapeño peppers and sugar.

To make the lake trout in foil: Preheat the oven to 400°F (200°C).

In a large bowl, toss together the mushrooms, fennel, melted butter, and thyme. Season to taste with salt and set aside.

Tear off a 30-inch (75 cm)-long piece of heavy-duty aluminum foil. Place the mushroom mixture in the center of the foil. Lay the lemon slices over the mushroom mixture and place the lake trout on top of the lemon. Tightly wrap the foil over the fish and mushrooms and place the sealed packet on a sheet pan. Bake for 25 to 30 minutes until the fish reaches 145°F (63°C) measured with an instant-read thermometer.

To serve: Carefully open the foil packet. Top with some of the sugar-cured jalapeños and let your guests dig in!

SMOKED TROUT– STUFFED PUDGY PIE HASH BROWNS

Pudgy pie makers (two tiny cast-iron pans on the end of two long roasting sticks) are the most versatile pieces of cooking equipment you can use over a campfire. From breakfast to dinner, you can pretty much place anything you want in the cookers and make a good meal. This is an easy breakfast recipe that takes your basic hash browns and stuffs them with smoked trout. You may run into some issues with the potatoes sticking to the pudgy pie maker, so make sure the cooker is well seasoned. You'll also want to make sure it's warm when you add the butter and that you've squeezed as much water from the potatoes as possible. If you don't have butter, nonstick cooking spray works well, too. Feel free to open the cooker multiple times during cooking to see how the potatoes are browning. Top with an egg and you have a perfect campfire breakfast. If you want to step it up, add some hollandaise sauce!

YIELD: Serves 4

INGREDIENTS

4 large russet potatoes, peeled and grated

2 teaspoons kosher salt

4 tablespoons (56 g) cold unsalted butter

12 ounces (340 g) smoked or roasted trout or salmon (leftovers work well)

4 large eggs

PROCEDURE

Start an open fire with whole logs or in a grill, and let it get hot, until there's a good coal base and the fire is burning strong (see page 23) before starting this recipe.

Place the grated potatoes in a large bowl. Cover them with cold water and pour out the water. Do this a few times until the water is clear and the potatoes aren't releasing any more starch. Drain the potatoes and squeeze out as much liquid as possible. Dry the bowl and return the drained potatoes to it. Add 2 teaspoons of kosher salt.

Rub the cold butter on the inside of the pudgy pie maker until there's a thin coating. Warm your pudgy pie maker directly over the fire until it is hot enough to melt the butter, about 2 minutes. Tip the pudgy pie maker around to spread the butter until melted and the pudgy pie maker is coated.

recipe continues

NOTE

If you're not planning on keeping your catch, catch-and-release fishing is an equally rewarding experience. When practicing catch-and-release fishing, do your best to stress the fish as little as possible, giving it a higher chance for survival. Work quickly to remove hooks and get the fish back into the water as fast as possible!

To each side of the pudgy pie maker, add a tightly packed layer of potatoes. Place 2 to 3 ounces (28 to 42 g) of trout in the middle of the potatoes on one side only. Close the pudgy pie maker and place it over the fire. Cook, flipping and turning, until the hash browns are browned, 6 to 8 minutes total, checking after 3 to 4 minutes and then every 2 minutes or so to ensure they don't burn.

Once the hash browns are done, heat a large skillet over the fire right on the wood. Add a dollop of butter to melt. Crack the eggs into the skillet and cook them, sunny-side up, for 4 to 6 minutes until the whites are set, holding the pan closer or farther from the heat, as needed, making sure not to burn the eggs.

Remove the hash browns from the pudgy pie maker while the eggs finish cooking and place them on plates. Top with the fried eggs and serve.

STEELHEAD TROUT QUICHE
with Fiddleheads, Morels, and Arugula

Steelhead trout and eggs are one of those timeless combinations that pleases just about everyone. Turning that combination into quiche amplifies the feeling of a homey, down-to-earth meal. Beyond that, this dish screams springtime with the arrival of steelhead and fiddlehead ferns.

There are two ways to make this dough: I do it the simple way, baking the quiche only one time. If you want a crispier crust, blind bake the crust (fill the crust with parchment and dried beans and bake until crisp, about 10 minutes) before adding the eggs. You can also take a shortcut and buy a premade pie shell.

YIELD: Serves 4 to 6

INGREDIENTS FOR THE DOUGH

1½ cups (186 g) all-purpose flour, plus more for the work surface

12 tablespoons (1½ sticks, or 168 g) cold unsalted butter, thinly sliced

Pinch kosher salt

⅓ cup (80 ml) ice water

INGREDIENTS FOR THE SALAD

¼ cup (56.25 g) ramp bottoms, thinly sliced

Juice of 1 large lemon

1 tablespoon (15 ml) grapeseed oil

Kosher salt

One 12-ounce (340 g) bag baby arugula

1 cup (100 g) fiddlehead ferns, blanched

PROCEDURE

To make the dough: In a large bowl, combine the flour, cold butter, and salt. Working quickly, crumble the butter into the flour by rubbing it between your clean hands. A little at a time, add the ice water and mix the dough until it starts to come together. The dough should stick together easily, but it shouldn't be extremely wet. Add just enough water so it's not crumbling, but still sticks together with ease. (Alternatively, you can do this in a food processor.) Divide the dough in half.

On a lightly floured surface, roll out one of the halves to about ⅛ inch (0.3 cm) thick. Place the rolled dough onto a sheet pan and refrigerate for 1 to 2 hours until completely chilled. Tightly wrap the remaining dough in plastic wrap and refrigerate for up to 3 days or freeze for up to 1 month for future use.

While the dough chills, make the salad: In a large nonreactive bowl, combine the ramp bottoms and lemon juice. Set aside for 1 hour to marinate. Whisk in the grapeseed oil and a pinch of salt. Add the arugula and fiddleheads. Toss to coat in the dressing.

recipe continues

INGREDIENTS FOR THE FILLING

1 tablespoon (14 g) unsalted butter, plus more for preparing the pie plate

1 small shallot, diced

2 garlic cloves, sliced

1½ cups (99 g) cleaned and halved morel mushrooms

Kosher salt

1 cup (225 g) loosely packed diced ramp tops

8 ounces (225 g) leftover smoked or roasted steelhead trout, shredded

6 large eggs

1 cup (240 ml) heavy cream

Freshly ground black pepper

To make the filling: In a large sauté pan or skillet over medium heat, melt the butter. Add the shallot and garlic. Slowly sweat them until softened, about 5 minutes. Add the mushrooms and a pinch of salt. Cook until the mushrooms are soft, about 4 minutes, stirring occasionally. Add the ramps. Cook for 1 minute. Remove the pan from the heat and let cool to room temperature. Add the trout.

In a large bowl, combine the eggs and heavy cream. Using a fork, beat until completely combined. Season to taste with salt and pepper.

Preheat the oven to 350°F (180°C). Generously coat a glass pie plate with butter.

Remove the rolled dough from the refrigerator and place it into the prepared pie plate. Form the dough to fit the plate, removing any extra dough hanging over the edge. Spread the mushroom and trout mix into the dough. Pour the egg mixture over the top. Bake for about 30 minutes, or until the eggs are cooked and the quiche just starts to develop some color. Remove from the oven and set aside.

To serve: Cut the quiche into 4 to 6 slices. Place one piece on each plate and add a handful of salad on the side. Drizzle the quiche with any ramp vinaigrette left in the bowl.

NEWSPAPER TROUT

I can almost guarantee this recipe was first made by someone who had only newspaper and a few trout sitting next to a campfire. Great recipes are often made with a lack of ingredients—forcing you to use what you have around you—and I think this is one of those scenarios. At its core, this recipe is as minimalistic as it comes . . . well, that is, without the addition of the radicchio salad and maple vinaigrette. The bitter greens go well with the sweetened vinaigrette and add a flavor pop to the fish. You can use any type of trout, just adjust the cooking time and the amount of paper—the bigger the fish, the more paper you'll need and the longer to cook. I used a large lake trout for this recipe and about two sections of the newspaper. You'll also need parchment paper and butcher's twine. Although I cooked this fish in the oven, this recipe translates well to a grill or over an open fire.

YIELD: Serves 6 to 8

INGREDIENTS FOR THE TROUT

One 3- to 4-pound (1.35 to 1.8 kg) lake trout, gutted and scaled

Kosher salt

Freshly ground black pepper

1 bunch fresh flat-leaf parsley

1 lemon, sliced

INGREDIENTS FOR THE SALAD

2 large heads radicchio, quartered through the root end so they stay intact

Grapeseed oil, for coating the radicchio

Kosher salt

½ cup (58 g) chopped oil-packed sun-dried tomatoes, drained, oil reserved for the vinaigrette

½ cup (68 g) toasted pine nuts

PROCEDURE

To make the trout: Preheat the oven to 450°F (230°C).

Season the trout with salt and pepper. Stuff the fish's cavity with the parsley and lemon slices.

Lay out newspaper so it's about 6 inches (15 cm) larger than your fish on both sides and about 10 layers deep. Place a layer of parchment paper over the newspaper. Lay the stuffed trout in the middle of the paper and wrap the paper around the fish, fully covering it. Using butcher's twine, tightly tie the newspaper around the fish in 5 or 6 places, depending on the size of the fish.

Fill a clean sink with cold water. Place the newspaper-wrapped fish into the sink and let soak for 2 to 3 minutes. Remove the packet from the water and place it on a sheet pan. Roast for about 45 minutes, or until the fish reaches an internal temperature of 145°F (63°C) measured with an instant-read thermometer.

While the fish cooks, make the salad: Heat a large skillet over medium-high heat. Lightly oil the cut sides of the radicchio with grapeseed oil and season with salt. Working in small batches so you don't crowd the skillet, add the radicchio to the hot skillet, cut side down, and sear for about 30 seconds on each cut side, or until they begin to brown. The radicchio should have some crunch left to it. Once all the radicchio is browned, set aside to cool to room temperature. Once cooled, chop into 1-inch (2.5 cm) cubes and transfer to a large bowl. Stir in the sun-dried tomatoes and toasted pine nuts.

recipe continues

INGREDIENTS FOR THE VINAIGRETTE

3 tablespoons (45 ml) grapeseed oil

3 tablespoons (45 ml) reserved sun-dried tomato oil

2 tablespoons (30 ml) apple cider vinegar

1 medium shallot, minced

Kosher salt

To make the vinaigrette: In a medium bowl, combine all the vinaigrette ingredients and season to taste with salt. Whisk thoroughly to combine. Add just enough dressing to the radicchio to coat it, saving some for the fish. Toss to coat the salad.

To serve: Unwrap the newspaper from the trout and peel away the skin. Pick the flesh off the bones and serve with a scoop of the dressed salad. Drizzle the fish with some of the remaining vinaigrette and serve.

FIRE-ROASTED TROUT
on Avocado Toast

I'm a huge fan of cooking things on sticks over an open fire. The simplicity of the process plus the depth of flavor it brings to meat makes it a go-to cooking technique for me. This recipe pairs trout smoked over an open fire with a clean, bright avocado toast with sweet and spicy jalapeños. I don't think I could imagine a better meal to start a day.

YIELD: Serves 4 to 6 as a snack

INGREDIENTS FOR THE TROUT

One 1-pound (454 g) rainbow or brown trout, scaled and gutted

Kosher salt

INGREDIENTS FOR THE AVOCADO TOAST

4 ripe avocados, halved and pitted

Juice of 2 limes

Kosher salt

1 loaf artisan whole-grain wheat bread, sliced

1 recipe Sugar-Cured Jalapeños (page 61; optional)

PROCEDURE

Start a fire in your grill with hardwood or lump charcoal (see page 23), making sure the fire has a good, hot, coal base.

To make the trout: Find a green wooden stick about ½ inch (1 cm) wide and long enough to hold over a fire comfortably without burning your hands. Position the trout's stomach cavity around the stick. If it's clumsily on there, cut a little farther down into the tail so it can rest comfortably on the stick. Using 4 to 5 pieces of butcher's twine, securely tie the fish around the stick. Season the fish with salt. Place the fish over the fire, rotating it so it cooks evenly. Aim to get the skin a bit crispy and cook it until the meat is just cooked through, 10 to 15 minutes, depending on how hot your fire is. Once it reaches 145°F (63°C) when measured with an instant-read thermometer, set the fish aside to rest.

While the fish rests, make the avocado toast: Scoop the avocado flesh into a medium bowl. Add the lime juice and season to taste with salt. Using a fork, mash the avocados.

Toast the bread.

To serve: Spread the avocado mash over the toast and flake some of the trout onto each piece. Garnish with the sugar-cured jalapeños (if using) and serve.

photos continue

WALLEYE & NORTHERN PIKE

RECIPES

SALT DOME WALLEYE
Lettuce Wraps

◇

If I was able to cook everything underneath a giant dome of salt, I'm pretty sure that'd be the only way I'd cook. Creating a dome of salt gives the fish a higher salinity level, but it also traps in all the moisture and produces a soft, buttery texture that's hard to create using any other method.

You can serve this with anything you like, but here you'll find everything you need—I make the accoutrements from scratch, but, admittedly, it is a lot of work! Feel free to use store-bought sauces or slaws. I'd recommend having something savory, something acidic, something crunchy, something spicy, and something fresh. Any combination of those characteristics equals tasty wraps! This makes a light, flavorful snack that can be eaten over the course of an afternoon.

YIELD: Serves 6 to 8; makes 1 quart (760 g) coleslaw, 2 cups (480 ml) sweet and sour sauce, 2 cups (300 g) quick cucumber pickles, and 1 cup (180 g) simmered peppers

INGREDIENTS FOR THE WALLEYE

6 pounds (2.7 kg) kosher salt

4 large egg whites

½ cup plus 1 tablespoon (135 ml) water

Two 1½- to 2½-lb (679 g to 1.1 kg) walleyes, gutted and scaled

1 lemon, sliced

25 Bibb lettuce leaves

1 cup (125 g) chopped toasted cashews

INGREDIENTS FOR THE RED CABBAGE COLESLAW

½ head red cabbage, shredded

1 teaspoon kosher salt

1 tablespoon (15 ml) rice wine vinegar

½ teaspoon ground aniseed

PROCEDURE

I use a wood-fired oven for this and get it to an internal temperature of 600°F (315.5°C). If using a conventional oven, get it as hot as possible.

To make the walleye: In a large bowl, combine the salt, egg whites, and water. Mix until well combined.

On a sheet pan, lay a ½-inch (1 cm) layer of the salt mixture. Place the walleyes on top of the salt and stuff the cavities of the walleyes with the lemon slices. Using the remainder of the salt mixture, form a dome around the walleyes so they're completely covered. Pack the salt in so the dome doesn't have any open spaces. It should cover all of the walleyes. Bake for 45 to 50 minutes. You'll notice the salt start to brown and harden, which is a sure sign the fish is done, or almost done. If you're unsure whether it's cooked, leave it in the oven for about 10 minutes longer. Once the dome is brown and hard, remove the fish from the oven and set aside.

While the fish cooks, make the red cabbage coleslaw: In a large bowl, toss the shredded cabbage with the salt. Stir in the vinegar and let sit at room temperature for 1 hour. Sprinkle with the aniseed before serving.

recipe continues

INGREDIENTS FOR THE SWEET AND SOUR SAUCE

1¼ cups (300 ml) pineapple juice

½ cup (120 g) packed light brown sugar

½ cup (120 ml) apple cider vinegar

1 tablespoon (15 ml) soy sauce

1 tablespoon (8 g) cornstarch

2 tablespoons (30 ml) water

INGREDIENTS FOR THE QUICK CUCUMBER PICKLES

1 English cucumber, thinly sliced

Pinch kosher salt

½ cup (120 ml) rice vinegar

½ cup (120 ml) water

INGREDIENTS FOR THE SIMMERED PEPPERS

1½ cups (225 g) sliced mixed peppers (use a variety, hot or sweet depending on your palate, such as jalapeño, Thai chile, bell, or habanero)

1 cup (240 ml) water

½ cup (100 g) granulated sugar

½ cup (120 ml) apple cider vinegar

2 garlic cloves, thinly sliced

2 whole cloves

Pinch kosher salt

To make the sweet and sour sauce: In a 2-quart (1.9 L) saucepan over medium heat, combine the pineapple juice, brown sugar, vinegar, and soy sauce. Stir to combine and bring to a simmer for 2 minutes.

In a small bowl, whisk the cornstarch and water until smooth. Add this slurry to the simmering liquid, whisking until it thickens. Keep warm until needed.

To make the quick cucumber pickles: Place the cucumber slices in a medium bowl and sprinkle with the salt. Let sit for 30 minutes.

Squeeze the cucumbers to get rid of their water and return them to the bowl. Add the vinegar and water. Let sit at room temperature until needed.

To make the simmered peppers: In a 2-quart (1.9 L) saucepan over medium heat, combine the sliced peppers, water, sugar, vinegar, garlic, whole cloves, and salt. Simmer until the peppers soften, about 1 minute. Remove from the heat and let cool to room temperature. Remove and discard the whole cloves before serving.

To serve: Using a clean hammer, crack open the salt dome and pull away the chunks of salt. Remove the walleyes from the salt and brush away as much salt as possible from the outside and the cavity of the fish. Place them onto a cutting board. Remove the walleye skins.

On another board, arranged the lettuce leaves and all the accoutrements. Place the toasted cashews in a small bowl. Assemble your lettuce wraps with whatever you like!

MUSHROOM-CRUSTED WALLEYE
with Sautéed Spring Vegetables

Crusting fish and other proteins is something I really love. The addition of dried mushroom adds savor to the dish and also gives pale-colored fish a shot of color contrast that creates a stunning presentation. This dish uses dried morels to crust the walleye, which echoes the flavors of the morels in the rest of the dish. As a complete dish, it screams spring with the addition of fava beans and asparagus.

YIELD: Serves 4

INGREDIENTS

Four 6-ounce (170 g) walleye steaks, patted dry

Kosher salt

4 tablespoons (16 g) finely ground dried morel mushrooms

Grapeseed oil, for cooking the fish

2 tablespoons (28 g) unsalted butter

3 shallots, finely diced

2 garlic cloves, thinly sliced

1 tablespoon (3 g) fresh thyme leaves

8 ounces (225 g) fresh morel mushrooms, cleaned of dirt and cut to an edible size, if needed

½ cup (120 ml) chicken stock

1 cup (125 g) thinly sliced (on a bias) asparagus

½ cup (75 g) fava beans, blanched and shelled

¼ cup (60 g) heavy cream

Freshly squeezed lemon juice, for seasoning

PROCEDURE

Heat a large sauté pan or skillet over high heat. Season the walleye steaks with salt. Coat one side of each steak with 1 tablespoon (4 g) of the dried morels. Shake off the excess.

Place enough grapeseed oil in the pan to lightly coat the bottom and heat it just until smoking. Place the steaks in the hot pan, morel side down, and decrease the heat to medium-high. Sear for about 2 minutes until the morels are crusted onto the fish. Flip the fish, decrease the heat to medium, and finish cooking the fish until cooked through, about 5 minutes more. Transfer the fish to paper towels to drain. Keep warm.

Wipe out the sauté pan or skillet and place it over low heat. Add the butter to melt. Add the shallots, garlic, and thyme. Cook until the shallots are translucent, 4 to 5 minutes.

Add the morels. Cook until they start to soften a bit and have a pleasant texture and flavor, 4 to 5 minutes. Add the chicken stock. Cook until reduced to a saucy consistency, 4 to 5 minutes.

Throw in the asparagus and fava beans and let them warm through. Add the heavy cream. Simmer until reduced by half. Season to taste with salt and lemon juice

Place a large spoonful of the spring vegetables on the bottom of a bowl with a bit of the sauce. Place a piece of walleye on top and serve.

WALLEYE AND WILD RICE SAUSAGE

This recipe comes from my friend Jack Riebel, an acclaimed chef and staple of the Minneapolis food scene. When I saw his walleye sausage recipe, I knew it had to be in this book. It's reminiscent of a lobster roll, but, with the addition of walleye, I think he's somehow improved on that. Catch Jack at the Lexington in St. Paul, Minnesota—he owns the joint, so he'll probably stay there—or make this recipe at home for a taste from his kitchen!

YIELD: Serves 6 to 8

INGREDIENTS

908 g (2 pounds) walleye fillets, skin removed

20 g (0.7 ounce, or about 1 heaping tablespoon) kosher salt

1 g (0.035 ounce) ground coriander

0.5 g (0.017 ounce) ground ginger

30 g (1 ounce, or about 3¾ tablespoons) cornstarch

4 large eggs

480 ml (2 cups) whole milk

82.5 g (2.9 ounces, or about ½ cup) cooked wild rice, roughly chopped

12 g (0.4 ounce, or ¼ cup) fresh minced chives

1.2 m (4 feet) natural sheep casings

2 tablespoons (28 g) unsalted butter, plus more for toasting the buns

6 to 8 brioche buns, buttered and toasted

NOTE

This recipe requires a sausage stuffer, food processor, instant-read thermometer, and precise scale.

PROCEDURE

In a food processor, blend the walleye into a paste, about 1 minute. Add the salt, coriander, ginger, and cornstarch. Pulse until fully combined. Add the eggs. Pulse until incorporated. Add the milk and blend until the mixture is homogenous. Transfer to a large bowl. Fold in the wild rice and chives. Tightly cover the bowl with plastic wrap and refrigerate to cool.

Once the mixture is chilled, use a sausage stuffer to place the mixture into the casings, portioning them to your liking. I recommend 3½ to 4½ ounces (100 to 115 g) per link.

Fill an 8-quart (7.7 L) soup pot with 3 inches (7.5 cm) of water and place it over medium heat. Bring the water to a low simmer. Add the sausage and cover the pot. Poach the fish until they reach an internal temperature of 150°F (65.5°C) measured with an instant-read thermometer. Remove from the poaching liquid and transfer to a plate. Chill immediately.

To reheat the sausages: In a large cast-iron skillet over medium-high heat, melt the butter. Add the poached sausages. Cook, searing on each side, for 4 to 5 minutes total.

Serve in buttered and toasted brioche buns. I like to coat the interior of the buns with a layer of Homemade Aioli (page 87), add some chopped romaine lettuce before adding the sausage, and then top it all with Sugar-Cured Jalapeños (page 61), Quick Cucumber Pickles (page 83), and fresh dill.

WALLEYE IN NAGE BROTH
with Fall Vegetables

When making nage broth, fish is gently poached in a lightly seasoned broth and the accompaniments are then cooked in the same broth, making for a very aromatic dish—one that's bright, refreshing, and leaves you feeling renewed. The saffron and ginger add unmistakable flavor and distinct color, but feel free to include other ingredients, such as clams or mussels, just before serving to make it your own. Use any vegetables you like in the broth, but I recommend sticking to vegetables that cook quickly. You want them to add some texture without imparting any overly heavy flavors.

YIELD: Serves 4

INGREDIENTS FOR THE NAGE BROTH

2 quarts (1.9 L) water, light fish stock, or clear chicken stock

¼ cup (60 ml) champagne vinegar

1 medium white onion, peeled and halved

3 garlic cloves, peeled

2 celery stalks diced (large size)

1 fennel bulb, halved

One 2-inch (5 cm) piece fresh ginger, peeled

1 tablespoon (5 g) coriander seeds

1 tablespoon (6 g) freshly ground black pepper

2 cardamom seeds

2 teaspoons saffron threads

PROCEDURE

To make the nage broth: In a 6-quart (3.8 L) soup pot over high heat, combine the water, vinegar, onion, garlic, celery, fennel, ginger, coriander, pepper, and cardamom seeds. Bring to a simmer. Decrease the heat to medium and simmer the broth, uncovered, for about 1 hour, or until it reduces to roughly 1 quart (960 ml). Add the saffron threads to the liquid and let steep for 5 minutes. Strain the broth through a fine-mesh strainer into a medium heatproof bowl. If using in the next couple of days, refrigerate the broth tightly covered.

To make the walleye and vegetables: In a large sauté pan or skillet over medium heat, bring the nage broth to a gentle simmer. Add the walleye steaks and return the liquid to a very gentle simmer. Cook for about 4 minutes, or until the steaks reach an internal temperature of 145°F (63°C) measured with an instant-read thermometer. Remove the walleye steaks from the pan and set aside.

INGREDIENTS FOR THE WALLEYE AND VEGETABLES

Four 6-ounce (170 g) walleye steaks

1 cup (62 g) snow peas, strings removed, cut on a bias

1 zucchini, diced into ¼-inch (0.6 cm) pieces

12 cherry tomatoes, halved

Kosher salt

¼ cup (9 g) small fresh basil leaves

1 lemon, halved (optional)

Add the snow peas and zucchini to the broth. Return the liquid to a simmer and cook for about 2 minutes, or until they just begin to soften. Add the cherry tomatoes and return the liquid to a simmer. Taste and season with salt.

To serve: Scoop a healthy amount of vegetables and broth into a bowl, centering them in a group so you have a place to put the fish. Put the cooked walleye on top of the vegetables and garnish with basil leaves. Finish with a squeeze of lemon juice, if desired.

PAN-ROASTED WALLEYE
with Warm Aioli

Warm aioli smothers the fish in a mouthwatering coating that makes it as succulent as anything I have ever tasted. We're going to use nage broth (page 84) and modify it slightly with the addition of aioli to create a completely different experience than the Walleye in Nage Broth with Aromatics (page 84), but using very similar ingredients. This dish is advanced, so take your time and don't become frustrated if it doesn't come out correctly the first time—it will still be delicious. While the ingredients listed will be enough for four servings, I advise making the aioli first and following the procedure for the fish, one serving at a time, until you get the hang of it. Note that homemade aioli is crucial, as the dish won't turn out right with something store-bought. You will have leftover aioli— save the rest for Walleye BLTs (page 92).

YIELD: Serves 4

INGREDIENTS FOR THE HOMEMADE AIOLI

Juice of 1 small lemon

1 garlic clove, finely minced

2 large egg yolks

1½ cups (360 ml) grapeseed oil

Kosher salt

INGREDIENTS FOR THE WALLEYE AND SAUCE

Grapeseed oil, for cooking the fish

Four 6-ounce (170 g) walleye steaks, skin removed, patted dry

Kosher salt

2 cups (480 ml) Nage Broth (page 84)

⅓ cup (45 g) diced carrots

⅓ cup (40 g) diced celery

⅓ cup (28 g) diced fennel

⅓ cup (53 g) diced onion

¼ cup (60 g) Homemade Aioli

1 tablespoon (3 g) minced fresh chives

1 tablespoon (4 g) minced fresh flat-leaf parsley

Lemon wedges, for squeezing

PROCEDURE

To make the homemade aioli: In a large bowl, combine the lemon juice and garlic. Let sit at room temperature for 1 hour.

Add the egg yolks and whisk to combine. While whisking continually, slowly pour in the grapeseed oil. Continue whisking until all the grapeseed oil is emulsified into the egg yolks. Taste and season with salt. Tightly cover with plastic wrap and refrigerate to chill.

To make the walleye and sauce: Pour enough grapeseed oil into a large sauté pan or skillet over high heat to lightly coat the bottom. While the pan heats, season the walleye steaks with salt. When the pan is hot, place one (or more) walleye steaks, skin side down, into the pan. Decrease the heat to medium-high. Cook for about 2 minutes. Flip the fish and let it finish cooking, 2 to 3 minutes more. Remove the walleye from the pan and set aside.

Drain the pan of oil and return it to low heat. Add ¼ cup (60 ml) of broth to the pan along with one-fourth each of the carrot, celery, fennel, and onion. Cook until the broth reduces to just under 1 tablespoon (15 ml). Remove the pan from the heat and let cool for 30 seconds.

Whisk 1 tablespoon (15 g) of aioli into the broth. Return the pan to very low heat if the sauce needs to reduce more. The aioli will separate if it gets too hot, so use a gentle hand. Separated mayo will have a greasy, unpleasant flavor.

Season with one-fourth of the chives and parsley and to taste with salt and lemon juice. Place the walleye on a plate and pour the warm aioli over the top.

Repeat with the remaining ingredients for the remaining servings.

BREADED WALLEYE
with Charred Jalapeño Tartar Sauce

Breaded and pan-fried walleye is a classic for a reason—and I don't see anything taking its place in the near future. This recipe has the iconic three-stage breading that provides a crunchy crust. The walleye is served with tartar sauce that gets a kick from roasted jalapeños. For the breading, I like to use panko bread crumbs and break them up a little finer. I find standard-issue bread crumbs to be too fine and panko comes in a bit coarse, so breaking it down a bit makes for the perfect compromise. If you make the aioli for the tartar from scratch (see Homemade Aioli, page 87), the entire dish will stand out even more!

YIELD: Serves 4

INGREDIENTS FOR THE CHARRED JALAPEÑO TARTAR SAUCE

1½ cups (340 g) mayonnaise, or Homemade Aioli (page 87)

2 tablespoons (18 g) diced charred jalapeño peppers (see tip)

1 tablespoon (10 g) minced shallot

1 tablespoon (9 g) minced cornichon

1 tablespoon (9 g) minced rinsed capers

1 teaspoon minced fresh dill

1 teaspoon minced fresh flat-leaf parsley

Kosher salt

Freshly ground black pepper

Freshly squeezed lemon juice, for seasoning

PROCEDURE

To make the charred jalapeño tartar sauce: In a medium bowl, stir together the mayonnaise, jalapeños, shallot, cornichon, capers, dill, and parsley. Taste and season with salt, pepper, and lemon juice. Tightly cover and refrigerate until needed.

COOKING TIP

To char the jalapeños: Preheat a gas or charcoal grill to high heat, between 450°F and 550°F (230°C and 290°C). Place the jalapeños on the hot grill grate. Cook until they're black and soft, turning as needed. Let cool. Peel away and discard the charred skin. Remove and discard the seeds and the stem. Dice the jalapeños as needed.

INGREDIENTS FOR THE BREADED WALLEYE

6 large eggs, beaten

1 cup (124 g) all-purpose flour

2 cups (100 g) panko bread crumbs, lightly crushed

1 tablespoon (3 g) fresh thyme leaves, finely minced

1 teaspoon garlic powder

⅛ teaspoon cayenne pepper

Eight 4-ounce (115 g) walleye fillets

Kosher salt

Freshly ground black pepper

Grapeseed oil, for cooking the fish

To make the breaded walleye: Place the beaten eggs in a shallow container and the flour in a second shallow container. In a third shallow container, stir together the panko, thyme, garlic powder, and cayenne. Season the walleye fillets with salt and pepper. Working one at a time, coat the fillets on both sides with flour, shaking off any excess. Dip the fillets into the egg, remove, and place into the panko to coat fully. Set aside.

Heat a large cast-iron skillet over medium-high heat. Add enough grapeseed oil to cover the bottom of the pan generously and let it heat until just before smoking. Working in batches, place a few walleye fillets into the hot skillet. Cook for 3 to 4 minutes until browned. Flip and cook until the other side is equally browned and the fish is cooked through, 3 to 4 minutes more. Transfer the fish to paper towels to drain and continue cooking the remaining walleye. Serve immediately with the tartar sauce on the side.

NOTE

This recipe requires a sausage stuffer, food processor, instant read thermometer, and precise scale.

WALLEYE BLTS

When tomato season rolls around, it's tough to beat the flavor of a ripe heirloom tomato. When paired with thick slabs of roasted bacon, homemade aioli, crisp lettuce, and fried walleye, you're in for a treat. The key to a good BLT lies in all the ingredients being the absolute best they can be, so don't skip any steps! Find some beautiful heirloom tomatoes at a local farmer's market and track down some good bacon. (My favorite is applewood smoked bacon from Nueske's, in the middle of Wisconsin!)

YIELD: Serves 4

INGREDIENTS

8 slices bacon

8 slices whole wheat bread, toasted

½ cup (115 g) Homemade Aioli (page 87)

8 slices heirloom tomato

4 large Bibb lettuce leaves

4 Breaded Walleye Fillets (page 90), pan-fried

PROCEDURE

To make perfect bacon, skip the sauté pan or skillet. You'll have much more evenly cooked bacon this way! Preheat the oven to 350° (180°C).

Place the bacon strips on a sheet pan. Bake for 8 to 10 minutes, or until they're cooked to your liking.

To assemble each sandwich: Generously slather 2 pieces of toast, each with 1 tablespoonful (15 g) of aioli. In this order from bottom to top, on one slice of toast, stack 2 tomato slices, 1 lettuce leaf, 1 walleye fillet, and 2 bacon slices. Top with the second slice of toast and serve! Repeat with the remaining ingredients.

NORTHERN PIKE DUMPLINGS
in Watercress and Pea Soup

Due to the bone structure of northern pike, you can often end up with some less-than-ideal fillets for cooking. This recipe solves that problem by grinding the meat to get rid of scraps that otherwise might not find a home—and it does so with style. These dumplings are soft, clean-tasting, and carry a great fish flavor. They're balanced by the peppery and brightly flavored watercress soup that boasts a bright green color enhanced by fresh spring peas. If you're looking for a more refined experience, strain the soup through a fine-mesh strainer. Personally, I say skip the straining and enjoy the chunky bits.

YIELD: Serves 4

INGREDIENTS FOR THE DUMPLINGS

1 pound (454 g) northern pike, cleaned

3 large eggs

1½ cups (360 ml) heavy cream

Kosher salt

INGREDIENTS FOR THE SOUP

1 tablespoon (14 g) unsalted butter

1 large yellow onion, diced

2 garlic cloves, thinly sliced

1 pound (454 g) russet potatoes, washed, peeled, and diced

1 quart (960 ml) clear chicken stock

Kosher salt

4 ounces (115 g) sugar snap peas, strings removed

8 ounces (225 g) watercress

1 lemon, quartered

Fresh tarragon leaves, for garnishing

PROCEDURE

To make the dumplings: In a food processor, blend the pike until it's evenly chopped into small bits and looks semismooth. Add the eggs. Continue blending for 1 minute more. Add the heavy cream and blend until the mixture is smooth. Season to taste with salt and blend one last time. Transfer the mixture to a bowl, cover, and refrigerate until completely chilled, about 1 hour.

To make the soup: In a 4-quart (3.8 L) soup pot over medium heat, melt the butter. Add the onion and garlic. Sweat the vegetables until soft, 4 to 5 minutes. Add the potatoes. Cook for 3 minutes. Add the chicken stock and bring the soup to a simmer. Simmer the soup for about 20 minutes, or until the potatoes are soft. Pour the soup into a clean container and refrigerate the soup base to cool.

In a large bowl, prepare an ice bath and place a strainer in it. Bring a 4-quart (3.8 L) saucepan full of water to a rapid boil over high heat. Add enough salt, about ¼ cup (75 g), to the water to make it taste like seawater. Drop in the peas and boil for about 45 seconds, or until they're brightly colored and starting to cook. Using a slotted spoon, transfer them into the ice bath to cool. Remove from the ice bath and refrigerate.

Add the watercress to the boiling water and blanch for 15 seconds. Using a slotted spoon, transfer to the ice bath to cool.

recipe continues

Lift the strainer from the ice bath to remove the watercress. Squeeze out any excess water. Transfer the cooled vegetables to a bowl and refrigerate to keep cool.

Working in batches, in a standard blender, blend the soup base and vegetables until smooth. Taste and season with salt, as needed. Transfer to a container and refrigerate while making the dumplings.

To finish the dumplings: Fill a wide 4-quart (3.8 L) saucepan with about 4 inches (10 cm) of water. Add 2 tablespoons (36 g) of salt to the water to make it taste like seawater. Place the pot over high heat and bring to a simmer. Decrease the heat to medium.

Using 2 tablespoons, form small dumplings of the pike mixture between the spoons. Place them into the salted simmering water and cook for about 2 minutes, or until firm and cooked through.

To finish the soup: While the dumplings cook, place the soup over medium heat to warm. When the soup and dumplings are ready, ladle some soup into a bowl and place a few dumplings into the soup.

Garnish with a squeeze of fresh lemon juice and a sprinkle of tarragon and serve.

NORTHERN PIKE COOKED IN BUTTER

with Stewed Tomatoes, Arugula, and Torn Bread

Gently cooking fish in a fat—in this case, butter—is an easy way to bring the delicate flavors out of it. The butter slowly cooks the fish while keeping its moisture locked in, giving it a buttery flavor. Place that on some fresh stewed tomatoes with olives and capers and you have yourself a nice little meal!

YIELD: Serves 4

INGREDIENTS

4 large tomatoes

1 tablespoon (15 ml) olive oil

2 garlic cloves, sliced

1 shallot, minced

2 tablespoons (13 g) minced Castelvetrano olives

1 tablespoon (9 g) capers, rinsed and drained

1 tablespoon (4 g) minced fresh oregano leaves

4 pounds (1.8 kg) unsalted butter

Four 8-ounce (225 g) pike fillets

Kosher salt

Freshly ground black pepper

4 handfuls arugula

¼ cup (60 ml) sun-dried tomato vinaigrette (see Newspaper Trout, page 71)

16 large croutons, preferably homemade

PROCEDURE

Bring a 4-quart (3.8 L) pot filled with water to a boil over high heat.

On the bottom of each tomato, using a sharp paring knife, cut a small X that just pierces the skin. Place the tomatoes into the boiling water for approximately 45 seconds, or until you see the skin start to peel away from the tomato where it was cut. Using a large slotted spoon, remove the tomatoes and run them under cool water until cooled. With a paring knife, peel back the tomato skins from where the X was made. Dice the tomatoes and set them aside.

In a large sauté pan or skillet over medium heat, combine the olive oil, garlic, and shallot. Cook for about 3 minutes until translucent. Add the diced tomatoes. Cook them down until most of the moisture has evaporated, about 10 minutes. Stir in the olives and capers. Sauté for 1 minute more. Sprinkle in the oregano. Remove the pan from the heat and set aside.

In a 4-quart (3.8 L) saucepan over medium heat, melt the butter and heat it to about 160°F (71°C) measured with an instant-read thermometer.

Season the pike with salt and pepper. Place a small metal trivet or silicone steamer rack into the butter so the fish doesn't lie on the bottom of the pan. Place the fish on the rack. Cook until it reaches an internal temperature of 150°F (65.5°C) measured with an instant-read thermometer, about 12 minutes. Using a slotted spatula, remove the cooked fish from the butter and place it on paper towels to drain.

Place the stewed tomatoes on a serving plate and top them with the fish.

In a large bowl, toss together the arugula, vinaigrette, and croutons. Serve the salad on the side.

BAKED NORTHERN PIKE
with Butter Beans and Bacon

This recipe requires a strong, flavorful broth, which is why I recommend one that's homemade. Roasting a chicken carcass, covering it in water, and simmering it for 4 hours will get you the stock that makes the difference in the dish, or use Basic Fish Stock (page 151). If you make your own chicken stock, keep the roasted chicken bones covered with 1 inch (2.5 cm) of water the entire time it is cooking. The broth is then simmered with aromatics, bacon, beans, and herbs, all of which make the broth taste even better and stronger. If you already have the stock on hand, this is an easy, delicious, quick meal.

YIELD: Serves 4

INGREDIENTS

4 thick slices smoked bacon, diced

2 shallots, diced

2 garlic cloves, sliced

2 teaspoons minced fresh thyme leaves

1 teaspoon finely minced fresh rosemary leaves

1 Thai chile, sliced

2 handfuls chopped kale

1 (15-ounce, or 425 g) can butter beans, drained

2 cups (480 ml) roasted chicken stock (see headnote)

1 tablespoon (14 g) unsalted butter

Four 8-ounce (225 g) pike fillets

Kosher salt

Freshly ground black pepper

1 lemon, quartered

PROCEDURE

Preheat the oven to 350°F (180°C).

In a large sauté pan or skillet over medium heat, cook the bacon until crisp, 4 to 5 minutes. Pour off most of the fat, reserving about 1 tablespoon (15 ml) in the pan. Add the shallots and garlic. Sauté until the shallots are translucent, about 5 minutes. Add the thyme, rosemary, and Thai chile. Sauté for 1 minute more.

Add the kale, butter beans, and chicken stock to the pan. Bring to a simmer and let cook for 1 minute. Add the butter and let it melt.

Season the pike with salt and pepper and place it into a 9 x 13-inch (23 x 33 cm) baking dish. Pour the broth and bean mixture from the pan over the fish. Bake for 20 minutes, or until the fish is fully cooked and reaches an internal temperature of 145°F (63°C) measured with an instant-read thermometer.

To serve: Scoop some beans with the fish into a bowl. Squeeze fresh lemon juice over the top and serve.

CILANTRO AND JALAPEÑO–CURED PIKE

Curing fish in this fashion is similar to the Salt, Sugar, and Dill–Cured Salmon (page 51), but the jalapeños and cilantro here add a distinct punch to the fish. It takes best to a lighter-flavored fish such as pike, but you can experiment with other fish, as you prefer.

YIELD: Serves 8 to 12 as a snack

INGREDIENTS

1 cup (300 g) kosher salt

¾ cup (150 g) sugar

6 jalapeños, stemmed, seeded, and grated

2 bunches fresh cilantro, roughly chopped, 1 cup (16 g) reserved for garnishing

3 pounds previously frozen (1.36 kg) skin-off pike fillets, cleaned

Tortilla chips, for serving

Crème fraîche, for serving

Fresh limes, for serving

PROCEDURE

In a small bowl, stir together the salt, sugar, jalapeños, and cilantro. Sprinkle one-third of the salt, sugar, and herb mixture over the bottom of a glass baking dish large enough to hold the fish comfortably. Place half the pike fillets, skin side down, in the dish. Sprinkle the flesh side with the same amount of the salt mixture. Place the remaining pike fillets, skin side up, on top of the first half. Sprinkle the remaining salt mixture over the top of the fillets. Cover the fish directly with plastic wrap and weigh it down with something weighty, but not too heavy—say, a six-pack of beer. Place them in the refrigerator. Flip and drain the fillets every 12 hours for 48 hours.

Wipe off any excess salt mixture from the fillets. Remove the skin and thinly slice the pike before serving on tortilla chips topped with crème fraîche, sprinkled with fresh lime juice, and garnished with cilantro.

 RECIPES

CRAPPIE, BLUEGILL & PERCH

PERCH BRANDADE

This dish is classically made with salted and dried cod, but it translates to fresh fish well. With perch, I skip the dried and salted part, use fresh fish, and love the result. It's then whipped with boiled potatoes, garlic, grapeseed oil, and cream and served over toast. You can eat this chilled on bread or you can broil it, cover it in paprika, and spread it over toast.

YIELD: Serves 4 to 6 as a snack

INGREDIENTS

1 pound (454 g) perch fillets, skin removed

1 cup (240 ml) grapeseed oil, plus more for coating the fish

Kosher salt

6 garlic cloves, peeled

8 ounces (225 g) russet potatoes, washed and diced

½ cup (120 ml) heavy cream

1 teaspoon minced fresh thyme leaves

1 tablespoon (15 ml) freshly squeezed lemon juice

8 to 12 slices baguette, toasted

PROCEDURE

Preheat the oven to 350°F (180°C).

Coat the perch with a bit of grapeseed oil and season with salt. Place the perch on a sheet pan. Bake for 7 to 9 minutes, or until the fish is fully cooked and reaches an internal temperature of 145°F (63°C) measured with an instant-read thermometer. Remove from the oven and refrigerate to cool.

In a 1-quart (960 ml) saucepan over low heat, combine the grapeseed oil and garlic. Lightly simmer the garlic for 30 minutes, or until soft. Don't let the garlic get black; it will get bitter. Remove from the heat and let cool. Once cool, remove the garlic and mash it. Return it to the oil. Set aside.

Bring a 2-quart (1.9 L) saucepan full of lightly salted water to a simmer over medium heat. Add the potatoes. Cook until soft, about 15 minutes. Strain.

In the bowl of a stand mixer fitted with the paddle attachment, combine the garlic oil, potatoes, and perch. Turn the mixer to medium speed and slowly add the heavy cream and thyme. Mix until combined. Taste and season with salt and lemon juice, as needed. Spread the brandade on the toast and enjoy.

PERCH AND POTATO CHOWDER

In my opinion, fish and potato chowder should focus on two things—the fish and the potatoes (okay, sure, and bacon). Yukon golds are my favorite potatoes for this recipe as they add a buttery flavor and also have great texture in a chowder. A few big handfuls of fish are added right at the end of the cooking process, and gently cooked to perfection, to add a perch flavor to the chowder.

YIELD: Serves 8 to 10

INGREDIENTS

8 ounces (225 g) bacon, diced

1 large yellow onion, diced

2 garlic cloves, sliced

2 tablespoons (6 g) minced fresh thyme leaves

2 pounds (908 g) Yukon gold potatoes, washed, peeled, and diced

2 quarts (1.9 L) chicken stock

1 cup (240 ml) heavy cream

2 pounds (908 g) boneless, skinless perch, cut into large pieces

Kosher salt

Freshly ground black pepper

Handful minced fresh chives

PROCEDURE

In a 6-quart (5.8 L) soup pot over medium heat, cook the bacon until crisp, 4 to 5 minutes. Drain the fat, reserving 1 tablespoon (15 ml) in the bottom of the pot. Add the onion, garlic, and thyme to the reserved bacon fat. Cook until the onion and garlic are softened, about 5 minutes. Stir in the potatoes. Cook for 1 to 2 minutes to warm. Add the chicken stock and bring the chowder to a simmer. Simmer until the potatoes are just soft, 15 to 20 minutes.

Add the heavy cream and bring the chowder back to a simmer. Add the perch. Cook the perch for about 5 minutes, or until it's fully cooked and reaches an internal temperature of 145°F (63°C) measured with an instant-read thermometer.

Taste and season with salt and pepper. Finish with the chives just before serving.

CRAPPIE ESCABECHE

This is a great dish to sit around the table and snack on with tortilla chips. Escabeche can be made with meats, veggies, or seafood that's sunk in a flavorful, acidic liquid to help impart flavors. This escabeche is full of spicy peppers and finished with a hit of allspice to give it some body. The recipe, as is, isn't overly spicy, but feel free to reduce the amount of hot peppers used, if you'd like. Personally, I'd add another two or three habaneros . . .

YIELD: Serves 8 to 10 as a snack

INGREDIENTS

Eight 4-ounce (115 g) crappie fillets

Kosher salt

Freshly ground black pepper

¼ cup (60 ml) grapeseed oil, plus more for coating the fish and cooking the vegetables

2 large shallots, diced

2 large garlic cloves, thinly sliced

1 habanero pepper, diced (optional)

1 jalapeño pepper, diced

1 poblano pepper, diced

1 carrot, diced

1 tablespoon (3 g) fresh thyme leaves

¼ cup (60 ml) water

¼ cup (60 ml) champagne vinegar

2 bay leaves

½ teaspoon ground allspice

Pinch minced fresh flat-leaf parsley

Juice of 1 lemon

Tortilla chips, for serving

PROCEDURE

Preheat the oven to 350°F (180°C).

Season the crappie fillets with salt and pepper and lightly coat them with grapeseed oil. Place the fillets in a baking dish and roast until fully cooked, about 7 minutes, or until it reaches 145°F (63°C) measured with an instant-read thermometer. Remove from the oven and let cool.

In a 4-quart (3.8 L) soup pot over medium heat, heat a splash of grapeseed oil. Add the shallots, garlic, diced peppers, carrot, and thyme. Cook until just softened, 3 to 4 minutes. Add the ¼ cup (60 ml) of grapeseed oil, the water, vinegar, and bay leaves. Simmer for 5 minutes. Add the allspice and remove from the heat. Let cool.

When cooled, flake in the crappie. Add the parsley. Transfer the mixture to a large bowl and sprinkle with the lemon juice. Let sit at room temperature for 1 hour, or refrigerate for 24 to 36 hours. Serve with tortilla chips.

PAN-FRIED CRAPPIE
with Wild Rice and Grain Salad

When it comes to crappie, keeping the fish whole and searing it helps keep in moisture and eliminates the waste you might get when butchering the fish. On top of that, the skin, when crisped, is as delicious as any other part of the fish. This recipe pairs crappie with a grain salad containing fresh herbs and radish that's brightened by a champagne vinaigrette. The grains in the salad can be cooked a day or two ahead to make for less work the day you serve this, but should be brought to room temperature before serving.

YIELD: Serves 4

INGREDIENTS

4 whole crappies, scaled, gutted, and patted dry (this helps crisp the skin and minimizes splattering when the fish goes into the pan)

Kosher salt

Freshly ground black pepper

8 lemon slices, plus more for seasoning the salad (optional)

12 sprigs tarragon

Grapeseed oil, for cooking

1 cup (165 g) cooked wild rice

1 cup (100 g) cooked farro

1 cup (100 g) cooked rye berries

4 radishes, thinly sliced

½ cup (70 g) diced seeded cucumber

1 teaspoon minced fresh thyme leaves

1 tablespoon (3 g) minced fresh chives

1 tablespoon (4 g) minced fresh flat-leaf parsley

1 recipe sundried tomato vinaigrette (page 71)

PROCEDURE

Heat a large cast-iron skillet over high heat.

While the skillet heats, season the cavities of the crappies with salt and pepper. Stuff them with the lemon slices and tarragon.

Lightly coat the bottom of the skillet with grapeseed oil and gently lay the fish in the pan. Decrease the heat to medium-high. Brown the fish on both sides, 4 to 5 minutes per side. Remove the fish when it is fully cooked and reaches an internal temperature of 145°F (63°C) measured with an instant-read thermometer. Place it on paper towels to drain while you prepare the salad.

In a large bowl, stir together the cooked grains, radishes, cucumber, and herbs. Add the vinaigrette. Stir to combine. Taste and adjust the seasoning, as needed. Give it a squeeze of fresh lemon juice to make the flavors pop, if desired. Place the salad on plates. Pull the crappie meat and skin off the body and place over the salad.

CRAPPIE TERRINES
with Marinated Cucumbers

Terrines can be a terribly challenging undertaking that involve multiple steps and a skilled hand. I'm glad to say this version is quick and rustic and won't take an entire afternoon to create. The fish is roasted in paper with lemons and other aromatics, then blended with butter and herbs and placed into pots. It's then covered with another layer of room-temperature butter and refrigerated for up to five days. That's it!

YIELD: Serves 6 to 8 as a snack

INGREDIENTS FOR THE MARINATED CUCUMBERS

1 English cucumber, halved lengthwise

2 anchovies, minced

1 small shallot, minced

1 garlic clove, minced

1 tablespoon (15 ml) champagne vinegar

3 tablespoons (45 ml) grapeseed oil

1 tablespoon (4 g) minced fresh dill

Kosher salt

Freshly ground black pepper

PROCEDURE

To make the marinated cucumbers: Start a fire in the grill with lump charcoal and heat to roughly 500°F (250°C; see page 23).

Place the cucumber halves, cut side down, on the grill grate. Grill for about 2 minutes until they have good grill marks. Remove from the grill and let cool. Alternatively, you can do this in a grill pan on the stovetop. Refrigerate until chilled. Cut the chilled cucumber into a medium-small dice and transfer to a medium nonreactive bowl. Add the anchovies, shallot, garlic, and vinegar. Let sit for 30 minutes.

Add the grapeseed oil and dill and toss to combine. Taste and season with salt and pepper. Keep refrigerated, for up to 5 days, until needed.

recipe continues

INGREDIENTS FOR THE TERRINES

Grapeseed oil, for cooking

2 lemons, sliced

Eight 3- to 4-ounce (85 to 115 g) crappie fillets

Kosher salt

Freshly ground black pepper

1 tablespoon (7 g) ground celery seed

2 cups (480 ml) melted clarified unsalted butter, at room temperature

2 tablespoons (8 g) minced fresh flat-leaf parsley

2 tablespoons (8 g) minced fresh dill

1 teaspoon freshly squeezed lemon juice

4 garlic cloves, minced to shreds

To make the terrines: Preheat the oven to 400°F (200°C). Line a sheet pan with parchment paper.

Coat the paper with a thin layer of grapeseed oil and place the lemon slices around the parchment paper. Lay the crappie fillets over the lemons and season the fish with salt, pepper, and celery seed. Cover the fillets with another piece of parchment paper. Bake for 10 to 12 minutes, or until the fish is fully cooked and reaches an internal temperature of 145°F (63°C) measured with an instant-read thermometer.

Flake the cooked fish into a large bowl. Stir in ⅓ cup (80 ml) of butter, the parsley, dill, lemon juice, and garlic. Taste and season with salt and pepper until you like the flavor. Place the crappie into a 6-ounce (90 ml) jar and tightly pack it down. Top the fish with ⅛ inch (0.3 cm) of butter and refrigerate to chill.

I recommend serving this over toast with the marinated cucumbers on the side.

COOKING TIP

Keep the clarified butter at room temperature so that it binds nicely with the fish when mixing. If it's too hot or too cold mixing will be more difficult.

BLUEGILL
with Ginger, Thai Chile, and Garlic Oil

Bluegills are another prime candidate for cooking whole (see tip). Scaling them rather than butchering can save a bunch of meat and the skin crisps up perfectly. If you have a hot grill and a pile of bluegills, this is a perfect and delicious way to cook them. Start with a clean grill with oiled grates and mix some wood chunks in with the charcoal for an additional flavor kick. You'll probably have leftover oil, which can live in the refrigerator for two weeks and is great on any protein!

YIELD: Serves 6 to 8

INGREDIENTS

1 cup (240 ml) grapeseed oil, plus more for coating the fish

10 Thai chiles, minced

One 4-inch (10 cm) piece fresh ginger, peeled and minced

4 garlic cloves, minced

16 whole blue gills, scaled and gutted

Kosher salt

Freshly ground black pepper

PROCEDURE

In a small saucepan over medium heat, combine the grapeseed oil, chiles, ginger, and garlic. Slowly cook until they just begin to brown, about 6 minutes, and immediately pull the pan off the heat.

Start a fire in your grill with a mix of natural lump charcoal and hickory chunks and let it get hot (see page 23). Alternatively, heat a gas grill to between 450°F and 550°F (230°C and 290°C).

Season the bluegills with salt and pepper and give them a light coating of grapeseed oil. Place the fish on the grill. Cook for 4 to 5 minutes per side until the fish is fully cooked and reaches an internal temperature of 145°F (63°C) measured with an instant-read thermometer and has solid grill marks. Transfer the fish to a plate. Remove the meat from the bluegills and serve with the garlic oil for dipping, or pour a little oil over the fish and serve.

COOKING TIP

When grilling whole fish, you want to move the fish as little as possible. Let the fish cook all the way through on one side before flipping it. This lets the skin release from the grates more easily and also forms a better crust on the fish. Aim for the darkest brown color possible without turning the skin black.

CHOPPED BLUEGILL AND CORN CHOWDER

Similar to the Perch and Potato Chowder (page 104), this recipe focuses heavily on its main ingredients. It's all about the corn at first, with the bluegill coming in at the last minute to add some depth of flavor. The corn and fish pair perfectly to make a satisfying late-summer or fall meal.

YIELD: Serves 6 to 8

INGREDIENTS

5 ears corn, shucked, kernels cut from the cobs, cobs quartered

1 tablespoon (14 g) unsalted butter

1 yellow onion, chopped

2 garlic cloves, sliced

1 jalapeño pepper, minced

2 medium Yukon gold potatoes, diced

½ cup (120 ml) heavy cream

Kosher salt

Freshly ground black pepper

Grapeseed oil, for preparing the sheet pan

2 pounds (908 g) skin-off bluegill fillets

1 tablespoon (4 g) minced flat-leaf parsley

1 lemon, sliced

PROCEDURE

In a 4-quart (3.8 L) soup pot over low heat, combine the corncobs with enough water to cover by 2 inches (5 cm). Simmer the cobs for 1 to 2 hours. Once the corncobs are soft and the broth is flavorful, strain the cobs from the water and reserve the resulting stock. Measure the broth and add enough cold water to equal 6 cups (1.4 L) of corn stock. Reserve and refrigerate ½ cup (120 ml) of the stock to thin the soup. Set the remaining stock aside.

Return the pot to medium heat and add the butter to melt. Add the onion, garlic, and jalapeño. Sweat the vegetables until translucent, about 5 minutes. Add the potatoes and corn stock. Simmer the chowder until the potatoes are tender, 15 to 20 minutes.

Add the heavy cream and corn. Cook for 5 minutes more, or until the corn is soft. Taste and season with salt and pepper. Remove the pot from the heat and let the chowder cool for about 30 minutes until it's safe to blend.

Working in batches, in a standard blender, blend the soup until completely smooth. If serving immediately, adjust the consistency, if needed, or cool overnight, thin with the reserved broth, and rewarm before serving.

About 15 minutes before you're ready to serve the soup, preheat the oven to 350°F (180°C). Lightly coat a sheet pan with grapeseed oil.

Place the bluegill fillets on the prepared pan and season with salt. Lightly coat the fillets with grapeseed oil. Bake for 10 to 12 minutes, or until they're cooked through and reach an internal temperature of 145°F (63°C) measured with an instant-read thermometer.

Flake the fish into a medium bowl. Stir in the parsley. Place a pile of the bluegill into a bowl and ladle warm corn chowder over the fish. Give the bowl of chowder a squeeze of fresh lemon juice and serve.

COOKING TIP

This chowder will thicken significantly overnight and improve in flavor. If you can, let it sit overnight before serving and adjust the consistency the next day. Because you're making corn stock for this chowder anyway, just save a little for the next day to thin the soup. If you don't have extra broth, water works just as well.

BLUEGILL EN PAPILLOTE

As I mentioned on page 61, fish *en papillote* is a classic French fish preparation that sounds fancier than it is. Similar to cooking in aluminum foil, cooking *en papillote* means cooking in parchment paper with some aromatics, wine, and vinegar. To serve, the paper is carefully opened in front of the guest, who is met with the fragrant aroma from the contents. It's a great preparation for fish that can be prepped ahead and chilled to make serving dinner guests a breeze.

YIELD: Serves 4

INGREDIENTS

2 carrots, julienned

2 zucchini, julienned

2 large shallots, julienned

2 garlic cloves, thinly sliced

8 sprigs thyme

4 teaspoons (20 ml) white wine

Eight 3- to 4-ounce (85 to 115 g) skin-off bluegill fillets

Kosher salt

2 lemons, sliced

4 teaspoons (18.6 g) unsalted butter

PROCEDURE

Preheat the oven to 400°F (200°C).

Cut four 24 x 16-inch (60 x 35 cm) pieces of parchment paper into large heart shapes, about the size of two footballs next to each other. Place one-fourth of the carrots, zucchini, shallots, garlic, thyme, and wine on the bottom of one side of a paper heart.

Season the bluegill fillets with salt and place 2 fillets on the vegetables. Place 1 teaspoon (4.7 g) butter and a few lemon slices on top of the fish and fold the paper over the top of the fish. Crimp together the sides of the parchment to seal the packet. Repeat the process with the remaining fish, vegetables, and packets. Place the packets on a sheet pan and bake for 15 minutes.

Remove from the oven and serve immediately, being careful of the hot steam when opening the packets.

RECIPES

CATFISH, STURGEON, MUSKIE & WHITEFISH

CATFISH TACOS
with Crema and Tomatillo Salsa

When making tacos, I try to make a bunch at once. It seems like you always manage to find a few more mouths to feed if you get a good round of tacos going. Here in Minneapolis, there's a Mexican restaurant that sells fresh masa and its improved the quality of my tacos infinitely. Check your local Mexican markets to see if they sell fresh masa. If not, making tortillas from masa flour or lightly grilled corn tortillas also work great.

YIELD: Serves 8 to 12

INGREDIENTS FOR THE TOMATILLO SALSA

2 pounds (908 g) tomatillos, husked

Grapeseed oil, for cooking

2 garlic cloves

1 small white onion

1 jalapeño pepper

2 cups (32 g) fresh cilantro leaves

Kosher salt

Limes, for squeezing

INGREDIENTS FOR THE TACOS

6 pounds (2.7 kg) skin-off catfish fillets

Tony Chachere's Creole seasoning, for seasoning the fish

2 pounds (908 g) Frijoles Charros (page 124), cooked and warm

36 taco shells

2 cups (480 ml) Mexican crema

1 quart (248 g) snow peas, blanched and sliced on the bias

1 recipe Sugar-Cured Jalapeños (page 61)

Limes, for squeezing

PROCEDURE

Preheat the oven to 400°F (200°C).

To make the tomatillo salsa: Place the husked tomatillos on a sheet pan. Bake for 15 minutes until they develop some color and have softened.

In a large sauté pan or skillet over medium heat, heat 1 tablespoon (15 ml) of grapeseed oil. Add the garlic, onion, and jalapeño. Sauté until softened, about 6 minutes. Transfer the vegetables to a large bowl to cool.

When the tomatillos are done cooking, add them to the bowl and let everything cool. Transfer the cooled mixture to a food processor and add the cilantro. Pulse to chop roughly. Taste and season with salt and lime juice. Set aside.

To make the tacos: Season the catfish fillets with a liberal amount of Creole seasoning.

In a large sauté pan or skillet over high heat, heat 1 tablespoon of grapeseed oil until it's just about smoking. Decrease the heat to medium-high. Working in batches, add the fish to the hot pan and cook until it's cooked through, about 7 minutes, flipping a couple of times. It's done when it reaches an internal temperature of 145°F (63°C) measured with an instant-read thermometer.

Place a scoop of hot beans on a taco shell followed by catfish, crema, snow peas, jalapeño, and tomatillo salsa. Squeeze on some lime juice. Repeat and enjoy!

BLACKENED CATFISH
with Corn Succotash

When corn is in season, embrace it. There are a thousand ways to make a delicious succotash; this one is all about lightly sautéing a bunch of farmer's market veggies and lightly seasoning them. Topping the delicious succotash with blackened catfish adds a punchy protein to what is otherwise a light dish. You'll find it balances perfectly.

YIELD: Serves 4

INGREDIENTS FOR THE BLACKENING MIX

3 tablespoons (54 g) kosher salt

1 tablespoon (8.5 g) smoked paprika

1 tablespoon (6 g) ground white pepper

1 teaspoon garlic powder

1 teaspoon onion powder

1 teaspoon mustard powder

1 teaspoon dried oregano

1 teaspoon dried thyme leaves

ingredients continue

PROCEDURE

To make the blackening mix: In a medium bowl, stir together all the blackening mix ingredients. Set aside until needed. Store any leftovers in an airtight container at room temperature for up to 6 months.

recipe continues

INGREDIENTS FOR THE SUCCOTASH

Grapeseed oil, for sautéing

1 large white onion

2 garlic cloves, sliced

1 tablespoon (3 g) minced fresh thyme leaves

4 ears corn, shucked, kernels cut from the cob

2 small zucchini, minced

1 cup diced green beans, blanched

1 large tomato, diced

Fresh basil leaves, torn, for garnishing

Juice of 1 lemon

Kosher salt

Freshly ground black pepper

INGREDIENTS FOR THE FISH

Four 6-ounce (170 g) catfish fillets

4 tablespoons (48 g) Blackening Mix (page 121)

To make the succotash: In a large sauté pan or skillet over medium heat, heat 1 tablespoon (15 ml) of grapeseed oil. Add the onion, garlic, and thyme. Lightly sweat until the onion is translucent (it should not brown), 4 to 5 minutes.

Add the corn. Gently cook until the corn just starts to soften, about 3 minutes.

Add the zucchini and green beans. Gently cook until they are tender, about 3 minutes.

Toss in the tomato to heat. Finish the succotash with torn basil and a squeeze of fresh lemon juice. Taste and season with salt and pepper. Keep warm while making the fish or reheat quickly before plating.

To make the fish: Season both sides of the fish liberally with blackening mix. Heat a large cast-iron skillet over high heat until it just starts to smoke. Add enough grapeseed oil to lightly coat the bottom of the pan and decrease the heat slightly. Add the fillets to the hot skillet. Let them blacken for about 3 minutes. Flip the fish and finish cooking, 3 to 4 minutes more.

To serve: Place the warm succotash on a plate and top with the blackened fish.

CATFISH CAKES

When you talk about satisfying comfort food and fish, fish cakes are always on the top of my list. The texture and flavor of catfish work perfectly in these cakes and go great with the spicy tartar sauce. Don't overmix the ingredients or you'll end up with a gummy cake! When mixed just right, it should melt in your mouth.

YIELD: Serves 4 to 6 as an appetizer

INGREDIENTS

1 pound (454 g) catfish, cleaned

Grapeseed oil, for preparing and cooking the fish

Kosher salt

2 cups (180 g) crushed salty crackers (about 18 crackers)

½ cup (115 g) mayonnaise (I recommend Hellmann's for this)

1 tablespoon (15 g) stone-ground mustard

1 jalapeño pepper, minced

1 small shallot, minced

1 teaspoon chili powder

1 large egg, beaten

All-purpose flour, for dusting

1 lemon, sliced

1 recipe Charred Jalapeño Tartar Sauce (page 88), for serving

PROCEDURE

Preheat the oven to 350°F (180°C).

Lightly coat the catfish with grapeseed oil and season with a small amount of salt. Place the fish on a sheet pan. Bake for 12 minutes, or until the fish is cooked through and reaches an internal temperature of 145°F (63°C) measured with an instant-read thermometer. Remove the fish from the oven, place it on a plate, and refrigerate to cool.

In a large bowl, combine the crushed crackers, mayonnaise, mustard, jalapeño, shallot, chili powder, and egg. Flake the cooled fish into the bowl. Using clean hands, gently mix the ingredients until fully incorporated. Tightly pack a ½-cup (120 ml) measuring cup (to help form the cakes evenly) with the mixture to form patties.

Heat a large sauté pan or skillet over medium-high heat. Add a thin coating of grapeseed oil to the skillet and heat until it just about starts to smoke.

Lightly dust the cakes with flour. Add them to the hot skillet and brown until warmed throughout, 3 to 4 minutes. Serve with a squeeze of fresh lemon juice and the tartar sauce on the side.

CATFISH TIKIN XIC
(Mexican-Style Catfish)

This catfish recipe was developed by my buddy Jorge Guzman, who has a few James Beard Award nominations under his belt. Every one of his dishes that I've tried has been dynamic, thought-provoking, culturally significant, and downright delicious. This recipe stems from his Mexican heritage and will leave any guest at your house speechless.

YIELD: Serves 6 to 8

INGREDIENTS FOR THE FRIJOLES CHARROS

2 quarts (2 kg) dried black beans

1 ham hock

½ cup (112 g) lard or butter

2 carrots, diced

2 celery stalks, diced

2 jalapeño peppers, diced

1 yellow onion, diced

1 Fresno chile, diced

1 tablespoon (10 g) minced garlic

1 cup (240 g) ketchup

1 cup (240 g) Dijon mustard

1 cup (225 g) packed light brown sugar

¼ cup (85 g) molasses

2 tablespoons (30 g) chipotle purée

1 teaspoon ground cumin

1 teaspoon chili powder

1 herb sachet (bay leaf, thyme, rosemary)

2 quarts (1.9 L) chicken stock, plus more as needed

Kosher salt

PROCEDURE

To make the frijoles charros: In a 6-quart (5.8 L) pot, combine the dried beans with enough water to cover by 4 inches (10 cm). Bring to a boil over high heat. As soon as they boil, remove them from the heat. Let soak in the warm water for 1 hour. Drain the beans in a colander and rinse them with cold water. Set aside.

In a 6-quart (5.8 L) soup pot over medium heat, combine the ham hock, lard, carrots, celery, jalapeños, onion, Fresno chile, and garlic. Sauté for about 6 minutes.

Add the remaining ingredients, except the chicken stock and black beans. Cook for 3 minutes.

Stir in the chicken stock and black beans. Cook for 1 to 2 hours, or until the beans are soft. If the beans get dry, add a bit more chicken stock. Taste and season with salt. Remove the sachet and discard the ham hock. Refrigerate overnight if using the next day.

COOKING TIP

Make the beans and onions a day in advance so you only have to worry about making the fish the day of serving. Beans and pickled onions take some time; this recipe calls for a lot of both, so you'll have some leftovers to use anywhere you'd like!

recipe continues

INGREDIENTS FOR PICKLED RED ONIONS

1 quart (960 ml) distilled white vinegar

1 quart (960 ml) water

Juice of 1 lime

1 tablespoon (9 g) peppercorns

1 tablespoon (5 g) coriander seeds

1 jalapeño pepper, halved lengthwise

1 sprig marjoram

Big pinch sea salt

Big pinch sugar

2 large red onions, thinly sliced

INGREDIENTS FOR THE FISH

Six 6- to 8-ounce (170 to 225 g) catfish fillets

4 dried guajillo chiles

½ cup (120 ml) freshly squeezed orange juice

½ cup (120 ml) freshly squeezed lime juice

½ cup (128 g) achiote paste

2 tablespoons (30 ml) distilled white vinegar

1 beefsteak tomato, charred and coarsely chopped

½ white onion, charred and coarsely chopped

10 garlic cloves, roasted

2 whole cloves, stemmed

⅛ teaspoon ground allspice

2 tablespoons (30 g) sea salt

2 tablespoons (30 ml) grapeseed oil

2 large banana leaves

Warm tortillas, for serving

To make the pickled red onions: In a 6-quart (5.8 L) saucepan over medium heat, combine the vinegar, water, lime juice, peppercorns, coriander seeds, jalapeño, marjoram, salt, and sugar. Bring to a simmer and cook for 5 minutes. Remove the mixture from the heat and let cool.

Cover and refrigerate for 24 hours, and up to 5 days. Drain the onions from the liquid before using.

To make the fish: Preheat a griddle, grill, or skillet over medium heat

Place the catfish in a baking dish large enough to hold all pieces.

Bring a kettle of water to a simmer over high heat. Place the guajillo chiles on the griddle. Toast them just long enough to get a little color on both sides, about 20 seconds per side. Transfer the chiles to a medium bowl and cover with simmering water. Let soak for about 10 minutes to soften. Remove the chiles from the water. Remove and discard the stems and seeds.

In a standard blender, combine the rehydrated guajillos, the orange juice, lime juice, achiote paste, vinegar, tomato, onion, garlic, whole cloves, allspice, salt, and grapeseed oil. Purée until completely smooth. Pour the marinade over the fish, turning it to coat. Cover the dish with plastic wrap and refrigerate to marinate for at least 30 minutes, and up to 6 hours

Preheat the oven to 450°F (230°C).

Remove the fish from the refrigerator and remove the plastic wrap. Lay your banana leaves out on a kitchen counter. Wipe both sides with a damp towel to clean. In a separate baking dish of similar size, lay the banana leaves on the bottom of the dish. Place the fish on the leaves and cover with the marinade. Fold the leaves over the fish to cover completely.

Bake the fish for 15 to 20 minutes, or until it reaches 145°F (63°C) measured with an instant-read thermometer. Remove from the oven and carefully open the banana leaves to allow steam to escape. Serve immediately with warm tortillas, pickled red onions, and black beans.

STEAMED CATFISH
with Northern Thai Coconut Curry

I grew up in a small city in Wisconsin that had a large Hmong community. They opened my eyes to a style of cooking I wouldn't otherwise have known, and I developed a deep appreciation of it. So, when Yia Vang of Union Kitchen hit the Minneapolis food scene, I couldn't have been more excited to try his food. His recipes are drenched in culture and have intense, full flavors that honor his cooking roots. They also look extraordinarily beautiful. Everything he makes turns into a memorable meal, and this is no exception. Serve with rice or sticky rice, if desired.

YIELD: Serves 4 to 6

INGREDIENTS FOR THE CURRY SAUCE

⅓ cup (50 g) minced lemongrass

½ cup (80 g) minced white onion

¼ cup (25 g) minced peeled galangal

¼ cup (25 g) minced peeled fresh ginger

¼ cup (34 g) minced garlic

4 kaffir lime leaves

2 roasted red bell peppers, diced

One 8-ounce (225 g) can crushed tomatoes

⅓ cup (85 g) red curry paste

⅓ cup (80 ml) grapeseed oil

2 quarts (1.9 L) coconut milk (I like Chaokoh brand)

Kosher salt

PROCEDURE

To make the curry sauce: In a large sauté pan or skillet over medium heat, combine the lemongrass, onion, galangal, ginger, garlic, lime leaves, roasted red peppers, and crushed tomatoes. Sauté for about 5 minutes.

Stir in the curry paste and grapeseed oil. Decrease the heat to medium-low. Cook until a brown crust forms on the bottom of the pan (be careful not to burn anything though), about 15 minutes.

Add the coconut milk. Simmer the curry for 15 to 20 minutes. Working in batches as needed, transfer the curry sauce to a standard blender and blend until smooth. Strain the sauce through a fine-mesh strainer into the pan and place it over medium heat. Cook until reduced to a stewlike consistency, about 10 minutes. Taste and season with salt. Keep warm over low heat while you cook the fish.

INGREDIENTS FOR THE FISH

2 teaspoons minced garlic

2 teaspoons minced peeled fresh ginger

2 teaspoons minced scallion

2 teaspoons minced shallot

2 teaspoons minced lemongrass

1 teaspoon fish sauce

1 teaspoon kosher salt

2 pounds (908 g) skin-off catfish fillets

2 large banana leaves

To make the fish: Preheat the oven to 400°F (200°C).

In a small bowl, stir together the garlic, ginger, scallion, shallot, lemongrass, fish sauce, and salt until fully incorporated.

In a large bowl, combine the catfish and spice paste, rubbing it over the fish to coat. Divide the fish between the banana leaves and wrap them tightly. Place the banana leaves into a 9 x 13-inch (23 x 33 cm) baking dish. Bake for 15 minutes, or until the fish reaches 145°F (63°C) measured with an instant-read thermometer. Remove from the oven and let cool for a few minutes before serving with the curry sauce on top.

STURGEON AND ROAST BEETS
with Yogurt, Grapefruit, and Arugula Salad

I used to cook a dish similar to this in New York City at one of my favorite restaurants. It was a crowd favorite, and I hope you like it as well. The steaklike texture and umami flavor the sturgeon brings works great alongside the bright yogurt, fresh grapefruit, and arugula.

YIELD: Serves 4

INGREDIENTS

Kosher salt

4 medium red beets

1 cup plain full-fat Greek yogurt

1 tablespoon (4 g) minced fresh tarragon leaves

1 tablespoon (20 g) honey

Four 6-ounce (170 g) skin-off sturgeon fillets

Freshly ground black pepper

Grapeseed oil, for cooking the fish

1 tablespoon (15 ml) champagne vinegar

4 handfuls arugula

2 grapefruits, peeled, supremes segmented, juice reserved

PROCEDURE

Preheat the oven to 400°F (200°C).

In a 9-inch (23 cm) square baking dish, place ½-inch (1 m) layer of salt. Place the beets on top of the salt. Wrap the dish in aluminum foil. Bake until the beets are cooked through, about 1 hour. Remove the beets, let cool enough to handle, peel, cut into eighths, and set aside.

In a small bowl, whisk the yogurt, tarragon, and honey until blended. Taste and season with salt. Set aside.

Season the sturgeon fillets with salt and pepper. Heat a large sauté pan or skillet over high heat. Add a coating of grapeseed oil to the pan and let it heat until it just begins to smoke. Decrease the heat to medium-high. Add the fillets. Sear for 3 to 5 minutes per side and continue cooking until they're cooked through to a temperature of 145°F (63°C) measured with an instant-read thermometer, 7 to 8 minutes total.

In a small bowl, toss together the beets and vinegar. Season to taste with salt.

In a medium bowl, toss the arugula with the grapefruit supremes and 2 tablespoons (30 ml) of the reserved grapefruit juice.

To serve: Place a large dollop of honeyed yogurt on a plate. Top the yogurt with a couple spoonfuls of beets. Place a piece of fish on the side and garnish with arugula salad.

GRILLED STURGEON
with Anchovy Butter and Rapini

Sturgeon is one of my favorites because it eats like a big, meaty, lightly flavored beef steak. The meat holds up well to grilling and can take on a lot of delicious flavors. For this recipe, I treat it like a steak, pairing it with my favorite condiment, anchovy butter, to give the dish more savor. Gently cooked rapini, broccoli, or broccolini completes the dish. The sauce is a pan sauce made with the anchovy butter and rapini. The recipe for the anchovy butter is more than you'll need, but it's worth making extra to have around the house for toast, or if you like extra in the sauce like I do. Don't be afraid of anchovies and definitely don't skimp on the butter sauce!

YIELD: Serves 4

INGREDIENTS FOR THE ANCHOVY BUTTER

16 tablespoons (2 sticks, or 224 g) salted butter, at room temperature

4 anchovies, boned

1 tablespoon (15 ml) freshly squeezed lemon juice

1 tablespoon (4 g) minced fresh parsley

1 tablespoon (9 g) capers, drained and chopped

1 small garlic clove, peeled

INGREDIENTS FOR THE FISH AND RAPINI

Four 6-ounce (170 g) sturgeon steaks

Grapeseed oil, for preparing the fish

Kosher salt

Freshly ground black pepper

1 pound (454 g) rapini or broccoli or similar, blanched in salted water, drained

1 lemon, for squeezing

¼ cup (25 g) fresh bread crumbs, toasted

PROCEDURE

To make the anchovy butter: In a food processor, combine all the ingredients. Blend until combined. Reserve 4 tablespoons (56 g) and transfer the remainder to an airtight container. Refrigerate for up to 2 weeks.

To make the fish and rapini: Start a fire in your grill with a combination of natural lump charcoal and chunks of hardwood and let it heat to roughly 500°F (250°C; see page 23).

Brush the sturgeon steaks with grapeseed oil and season with salt and pepper. Place the steaks on the grill. Cook for 3 to 4 minutes per side until just done. Set in a warm space near the grill to keep warm.

In a large sauté pan or skillet over medium-high heat, combine the rapini with 2 to 3 tablespoons (30 to 45 ml) of water. Cook the rapini until it's hot throughout and transfer to a plate, reserving 1½ tablespoons (23 ml) of the cooking water in the pan. Return the skillet to medium heat.

Add the reserved anchovy butter and let it gently melt, slowly whisking so the water and butter don't separate. Place the rapini back into the pan and toss to coat. Season to taste with salt.

Plate the sturgeon steaks on a plate and pour the rapini and butter sauce over them. Add a squeeze of fresh lemon juice to the fish and sprinkle with the toasted bread crumbs to finish.

MUSKIE

A bit on eating muskies: Keeping and eating muskies can be a controversial subject. We caught the muskie used in these recipes on a Northern Wisconsin lake that, according to the head of the Department of Natural Resources for that lake, has an exuberant muskie population that could be helped by removing a few now and then. This particular muskie also had what appeared to be a previously broken spine and some battle wounds—all of which deemed it a good fish to keep and eat. Beyond being in a heavily muskie-populated lake, the fish itself wasn't as healthy as we usually see. Keeping this fish wasn't taken lightly, and every bit was eaten.

When keeping muskies, please check your local lake regulations and, with any fish, keep the overall fish population in mind. There are also considerations with young children, high-risk health populations, women of childbearing years, nursing mothers, and children younger than age 15—all should be cautious when eating apex predators (see page 19 for more information).

WOOD-FIRED MUSKIE NUGGETS

I haven't eaten that much muskie, but this is a muskie recipe I have enjoyed the most. It came about when I was trying to figure out different ways to incorporate a smoke flavor into the meat without cooking it for an extended amount of time. The end result was muskie cooked over wood on a sharpened juniper stick. It worked perfectly, as muskie responds well to a quick cook and also benefits from a solid smoke flavor. It's finished with a bright shallot and oil sauce to give it back some moisture.

Muskie, like northern pike, has a lot of Y bones to poke through during the butchering process. I use what I like to call a "five fillet" technique to make eating these fish easier (see page 36). For this recipe I used the top fillet, which dices into perfect squares that fit nicely on a stick.

NOTE: You will need a stick for this recipe for roasting. Find one long enough to hold over a fire pit and clean about 10 inches (25 cm) off it to a small point.

recipe continues

YIELD: Serves 6 to 8 as a snack

INGREDIENTS

1 shallot, finely diced

2 tablespoons (30 ml) apple cider vinegar

6 tablespoons (90 ml) grapeseed oil

1 tablespoon (7.5 g) chili powder

1 tablespoon (8.5 g) paprika

1½ teaspoons kosher salt

1½ teaspoons garlic powder

1½ teaspoons ground cumin

1 garlic clove, finely diced

One 16- to 20-ounce (454 to 568 g) muskie top fillet, skin removed and diced into ¾-inch (2 cm) pieces

PROCEDURE

Start an open fire with a combination of natural lump charcoal and/or hardwood, or in a grill, and let it get to between 450°F and 550°F (230°C and 290°C; see page 23).

In a small bowl, combine the shallot, garlic, and vinegar. Let sit at room temperature for 20 minutes. Whisk in the grapeseed oil until incorporated. Set aside.

Meanwhile, in a large bowl, stir together the chili powder, paprika, salt, garlic powder, and cumin. Add the muskie and rub to coat with the spice blend. Place the muskie cubes on the stick.

Hold the muskie over the fire. Cook for 6 to 8 minutes, rotating occasionally, depending on how hot the fire is, until cooked through and it reaches an internal temperature of 145°F (63°C) measured with an instant-read thermometer.

Pour the vinaigrette over the muskie and eat it right off the stick!

PICKLED MUSKIE

I love having pickled fish in the fridge. It's such a delicious grab-and-go snack! This recipe takes me back to my days working with Chef Paul Berglund, when we'd often get in a ton of fresh herring and needed it to last for a week—what better way to preserve some than by pickling? This recipe works great with muskie or northerns as well.

This pickle is a two-step process: The first is a mustard pickle to infuse a good amount of flavor into the fish and the second pickle cures the muskie while adding a heavy dose of acidity. The best part of this recipe is that it gets better every day that it sits in the second pickling liquid. Eat it on crackers, bread, or anything else crunchy you have in your cabinet. Add some Sugar-Cured Jalapeños (page 61) for an extra kick.

YIELD: Serves 8 to 12 as a snack

INGREDIENTS FOR THE FIRST PICKLE

2 cups (480 g) Dijon mustard

½ cup (120 ml) apple cider vinegar

1 tablespoon (18 g) kosher salt

2 pounds (908 g) cleaned and skinned muskie, diced (medium size)

INGREDIENTS FOR THE SECOND PICKLE

1 tablespoon (5 g) coriander seeds

4 allspice berries

4 juniper berries

1 medium red onion, diced

1 jalapeño pepper, diced

¼ cup (50 g) sugar

2 tablespoons (30 g) Dijon mustard

2 cups (480 ml) water

2 cups (480 ml) apple cider vinegar

PROCEDURE

For the first pickle: In a large plastic container, stir together the mustard, vinegar, and salt. Place the muskie into the mixture. Cover the container and refrigerate for 48 hours.

For the second pickle: In a 10 x 10-inch (25 x 25 cm) piece of cheesecloth, combine the coriander, allspice berries, and juniper berries. Gather the cloth in a bundle and tie it closed with butcher's twine. Place the filled cheesecloth and the rest of the ingredients into a 2-quart (1.9 L) saucepan and bring to a simmer over medium-high. Cook for 5 minutes. Transfer the pot to the refrigerator to cool, about 2 hours.

Once cooled, place the cooled brine in a glass container. Strain the muskie from the first pickle and place it into the cooled brine for at least 24 hours, and up to 7 days. It is ready to be eaten after chilling for 24 hours in the pickling liquid.

MUSKIE AND MUSSELS STEW

This is another muskie recipe I'm really excited about, as it combines the essentials of a tomato fish stew with muskie and mussels. The unique blend of seafood gives the stew a full-bodied broth that's hard to stop eating. It's great on its own, but you can also pour it over toasted bread to soak up all the tomato and fish goodness in the broth.

YIELD: Serves 6 to 8

INGREDIENTS

3 tablespoons (42 g) unsalted butter

2 medium white onions, diced

3 garlic cloves, thinly sliced

2 tablespoons (5 g) minced fresh sage

1 tablespoon (3 g) minced fresh thyme leaves

1 cup (240 ml) dry white wine

1 (14.5-ounce, or 410 g) can organic fire-roasted diced tomatoes

1 (2.25-ounce, or 64 g) jar capers, rinsed and roughly chopped

2 pounds (908 g) muskie, cleaned, diced (medium size)

1 pound (454 g) mussels, cleaned and debearded

¼ cup (16 g) chopped fresh flat-leaf parsley

PROCEDURE

In a 6-quart (5.8 L) soup pot over medium heat, melt 2 tablespoons of butter. Add the onions, garlic, sage, and thyme. Sweat the vegetables until translucent.

Add the white wine. Cook until reduced by half, 4 to 5 minutes.

Add the tomatoes and capers. Simmer for 10 minutes.

Add the chopped muskie and mussels. Cover the pot and cook until the mussels open, about 6 minutes. Discard any mussels that do not open. Add the parsley and serve immediately.

SMOKED WHITEFISH
and Thai Chile Salad

This is a craveable dish that combines whitefish, smoke, spicy chiles, and crunchy celery. With plenty of fat and flavor from aioli and crème fraîche, this is the star of any sandwich or snack plate. I must admit, I don't know what it is about this combination, but I can't stop eating it once I start. Serve it on salty crackers for an easy appetizer or pile it on toasted rye bread or a bagel for a substantial sandwich.

YIELD: Serves 8 to 10 as a snack

INGREDIENTS

2 pounds (908 g) smoked whitefish, free of bones (store-bought or smoked yourself; see tip)

⅓ cup (75 g) Homemade Aioli (page 86)

⅓ cup (75 g) crème fraîche

1 tablespoon (15 g) stone-ground mustard

4 Thai chiles, finely minced

3 celery stalks, minced

Handful minced fresh chives

Kosher salt

Freshly ground black pepper

1 lemon, for squeezing

INGREDIENTS FOR THE BRINE

1 gallon (3.8 L) water

1 cup (300 g) kosher salt

1 cup (225 g) packed light brown sugar

4 garlic cloves, peeled

10 pounds (4.5 kg) skin-off whitefish fillets

photo on page 117

PROCEDURE

In a large bowl, flake apart the whitefish. Lightly fold in the remaining ingredients until fully incorporated. Taste and season with salt, pepper, and lemon juice until your desired flavor is achieved!

To brine the fish: In a 6-quart (5.8 L) soup pot over high heat, combine the water, salt, brown sugar, and garlic. Bring to a boil. Pour the brine into a large plastic container (large enough to hold the fish and brine). Refrigerate to cool. Once cooled, place the fish in brine, cover the container, and refrigerate for 12 hours.

To smoke the brined fish: Remove the fish from the brine and place it on a sheet pan. Refrigerate the fish, uncovered, for 12 hours.

Once the fish develops a sticky outside texture, preheat your smoker to 145°F (63°C). Put the fish onto the smoker's grate and smoke for 2 hours until it reaches an internal temperature of 145°F (63°C) measured with an instant-read thermometer. Remove from the smoker and refrigerate in an airtight container where it will keep for 5 days.

COOKING TIP

If you purchase smoked whitefish, skip this. If you have whitefish to smoke, here's your guide! Whitefish, as do many meats, benefit from a 12- to 24-hour brine before smoking or cooking. After brining, let the fish dry, uncovered, in the refrigerator for 12 hours so it forms a pellicle (thin skin) that smoke will adhere to more effectively. I prefer smoking with red oak, but cherry, apple, or hickory hardwoods all work. If you have a pellet smoker, that works well, too. This is a very basic brine; feel free to add herbs or spices as desired.

SMOKED WHITEFISH
and Wild Rice Pancakes

I'll take a savory pancake over a sweet one any day. They're an underappreciated food in the world! This version includes smoked whitefish to give it extra oomph, and the wild rice adds some crunch. Instead of syrup, melt dollops of anchovy butter (page 132) over the pancakes and serve alongside eggs for a hearty breakfast.

YIELD: Serves 4 to 6

INGREDIENTS

1 cup (165 g) cooked wild rice

8 ounces (225 g) smoked whitefish, flaked (store-bought or smoked yourself, see page 140)

¼ cup (25 g) finely chopped seeded jalapeño peppers

1 cup (30 g) chopped fresh spinach

2 cups (248 g) all-purpose flour

2 teaspoons baking powder

1 teaspoon kosher salt

1⅓ cups (320 ml) whole milk

2 large eggs, beaten

2 tablespoons (30 ml) grapeseed oil

Unsalted butter, for cooking

PROCEDURE

In a large bowl, stir together the wild rice, whitefish, jalapeños, spinach, flour, baking powder, and salt

In another large bowl, combine the milk, beaten eggs, and grapeseed oil. Whisk to combine. Gently fold the wet ingredients into the dry ingredients, making sure not to overmix them. Form the batter into 6 to 8 individual patties and set aside.

Heat a large cast-iron skillet over medium-high heat and add a generous pat of butter to melt. Right before it starts to brown, working in batches and adding more butter as needed, add the patties to the skillet. Cook until browned on both sides and heated all the way through, 3 to 4 minutes per side. Serve immediately.

SMOKED WHITEFISH
and Soft Eggs on Rye

This recipe comes from another good friend of mine, Erik Sather. He's a local celebrity chef in the Twin Cities and owns and operates one of the best butcher shops I've ever been to, Lowry Hill Meats. They do stuff the old-school way there, breaking down whole animals and guiding customers through how to cook the different cuts of meat. He also cooks an entire menu of food there and, if you stop by, you might see this on the menu! He gets his whitefish from Northern Waters Smokehaus, another classic Minnesota staple on the North Shore.

YIELD: Serves 4

INGREDIENTS

6 tablespoons (84 g) unsalted butter

4 thick (1 inch, or 2.5 cm, or so) slices rye bread

8 large eggs, beaten until smooth and pale yellow

8 ounces (225 g) smoked whitefish (store-bought or smoked yourself, see page 140) lightly flaked apart, but still nice-sized pieces

4 ounces (115 g) Gruyère cheese, shaved into thin strips for melting

Sea salt

Fresh chives, for garnishing

Freshly ground black pepper

PROCEDURE

Place a large cast-iron skillet over medium-low heat. Using 3 tablespoons (42 g) of butter, butter the rye bread. Working in batches if needed, place the bread in the hot skillet and toast on both sides until golden but still soft in the middle. Remove the bread from the skillet and set aside.

Wipe the skillet clean with a paper towel, return it to medium heat, and add the remaining 3 tablespoons (42 g) of butter to melt, swirling the pan to coat it well. Pour in the eggs and let them sit for a moment. After about 90 seconds, while the eggs are slowly starting to cook but not brown, add the flaked fish and the shaved cheese. Lightly season with sea salt—the fish and cheese are already salty, so you just need to season the eggs.

Once the eggs start to cook, give them a gentle folding stir (we're not scrambling here) a couple times. Let them cook in the pan until mostly cooked, but still slightly runny, gently folding as needed. The residual heat of the cooked eggs will carry over and continue to cook the eggs on the plate.

Cut the toast in half and place it on a plate. Fold the eggs and fish one last time and top the toast with the mixture. Garnish with the chives and season with more sea salt, as needed, and pepper.

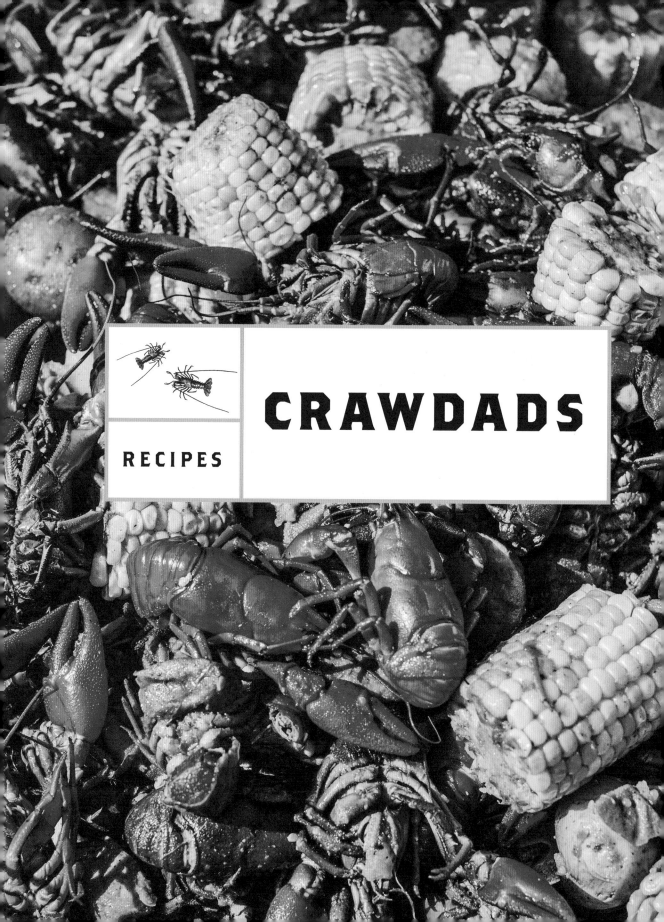

RECIPES

CRAWDADS

GRILLED CRAWDADS

When I'm cooking, I often draw inspiration from what's around me. For better or worse, one thing that's typically near me is some sort of smoker or giant grill. This recipe for crawdads, which is ideal for a larger gathering, embraces the grill by cooking sausage and corn in a pan right in the grill, then throwing the crawdads in and shutting the grill. This recipe uses the same ingredients as the Steamed Crawdads (page 149), but the results couldn't be more different. Everything here is covered in smoke and steam from the beer—stronger, more rustic flavors.

Before cooking 'dads, make sure they're properly cleaned. I use my (cleaned!) bathtub at home and rinse them in multiple batches of cold water until the water runs clean when they're rinsed. It usually takes 4 to 5 rounds of water.

YIELD: Serves 10 to 15

INGREDIENTS

Grapeseed oil, for cooking the kielbasa

2 pounds (908 g) kielbasa, cut into 1-inch (2.5 cm) chunks

10 pounds (4.5 kg) crawdads, cleaned (see headnote)

8 ears corn, shucked and halved

2 pounds (908 g) small potatoes, boiled until soft

Two 12-ounce (360 ml) bottles pilsner beer

Old Bay seasoning, to taste

PROCEDURE

Start a fire in your grill or smoker with a mix of lump charcoal and chunked hickory and get it wicked hot, to about 450°F (230°C; see page 23).

Heat a giant cast-iron skillet or paella pan on the grill and add a thin layer of grapeseed oil. Add the kielbasa. Sear the chunks until they have a solid brown color, 6 to 7 minutes total. Remove the sausages and drain the skillet of most of its fat, leaving just enough to coat the bottom.

In an extra-large bowl, stir together the seared sausage, crawdads, corn, and boiled potatoes. Place the mix back into the skillet and return it to the grill. Pour 1 bottle of beer into the skillet. Cover the grill and shut the top holes to about 50 percent. Let the mix steam and smoke for 10 to 15 minutes, or until the crawdads are cooked through and have reached an internal temperature of 165°F (74°C) measured with an instant-read thermometer, stirring the mixture once or twice to make sure everything is cooking evenly. Add more beer, if needed, to create more steam. Once cooked, remove the skillet and pour everything onto a paper-lined heatproof table. Aggressively season with Old Bay and dig in!

STEAMED CRAWDADS

This recipe stems from the way I like to cook crabs, which is a simple steaming. You'll find this is a clean-tasting, delicious meal that can please a huge crowd. As mentioned in the Grilled Crawdad recipe (page 146), it's important to clean your crawdads thoroughly before cooking them. That's doubly important in this recipe, where there's no smoke flavor to hide behind. To cook this just right, you'll need a large stockpot with a perforated insert that fits into the pot and sits off the bottom by about ½ inch (1 cm) or so.

YIELD: Serves 10 to 15

INGREDIENTS

Two 12-ounce (360 ml) bottles pilsner beer

10 pounds (4.5 kg) smoked crawdads (store-bought or smoked yourself, see page 146)

8 ears corn, shucked and halved

2 pounds (908 g) small potatoes, boiled until soft

2 pounds (908 g) kielbasa, cut into 1-inch (2.5 cm) chunks

Old Bay seasoning, to taste

PROCEDURE

In a 16-quart (15 L) stockpot over high heat, warm the beer.

In an extra-large bowl, combine the crawdads, corn, potatoes, and kielbasa. Transfer to the stockpot's insert. Place the insert into the pot and cover the pot. Turn the heat to medium. Let steam for 10 to 15 minutes, or until the crawdads are fully cooked and have reached an internal temperature of 165°F (74°C) measured with an instant-read thermometer. Remove the insert and pour the contents over a paper-lined heatproof table. Season liberally with Old Bay and enjoy!

CRAWDAD BISQUE

Bisque, like chowder, is the ultimate comfort food on a cold, rainy day. It's incredibly full-flavored, filling, and smells wonderful while it cooks. Make your own stock for this recipe—it's the game changer. As always, make sure your crawdads are clean and free of any dirt (see page 146) before you begin.

YIELD: Serves 6 to 8 as an appetizer

INGREDIENTS

3 pounds (1.36 kg) crawdads, cleaned

1 tablespoon (14 g) unsalted butter

2 celery stalks, roughly chopped

1 large carrot, roughly chopped

1 large yellow onion, roughly chopped

1 fennel bulb, cored and roughly chopped

1 head garlic, cloves separated and peeled

1 tablespoon (5 g) coriander seeds

1 cup (240 ml) sweet sherry

2 tablespoons (32 g) tomato paste

½ cup (95 g) long-grain rice

½ cup (120 ml) heavy cream

Fresh parsley, for garnishing

PROCEDURE

Fill a 6-quart (5.8 L) pot with water and bring it to a boil over high heat. Place the crawdads in the water and simmer for 4 to 5 minutes, or until they have fully cooked and reach an internal temperature of 165°F (74°C) measured with an instant-read thermometer. Using a slotted spoon, remove the crawdads from the water and set aside. When cool enough to handle, remove the meat from the tails and set aside. Using a cleaver, roughly chop the remaining shells.

In a 4-quart (3.8 L) saucepan over medium heat, melt the butter. Add the celery, carrot, onion, fennel, garlic, coriander seeds, and chopped shells. Sauté for 5 minutes. Add the sherry. Cook until reduced to just 1 tablespoon (15 ml), 5 to 6 minutes.

Stir in the tomato paste. Sauté for another minute to toast it slightly. Add enough water to cover everything by 2 inches (5 cm). Bring the mixture to a simmer and cook, mostly covered, for 2 hours without stirring.

Pass the stock through a fine-mesh strainer into a large heatproof bowl, pushing all the extra liquid through using the back of a ladle (that's the good stuff). Return the strained stock to the pot and bring it back to a simmer over medium heat.

Add the rice. Cook for 30 minutes, or until it's cooked through. Using an immersion blender, blend the mixture until smooth. Stir in the heavy cream and adjust for consistency, if needed (if too thick, thin with a bit of water; if too thin, let it reduce further).

In each bowl, place a pile of the crawdad tail meat and ladle the soup over it. Garnish with parsley and serve.

BASIC FISH STOCK

Fish stock is a great way to use up your carcasses and bones. Fish stock can be used in most fish recipes instead of water or chicken stock and in many soups and sauces. Like any stock, it's great to have a batch in the freezer for quick use.

YIELD: Makes 4 quarts (4 L)

INGREDIENTS

2 pounds (908 g) fish bones or carcasses, rinsed of any muck

2 celery stalks, sliced

1 large white onion, peeled and cut into 8 wedges

1 large leek, cleaned and sliced

4 thyme sprigs

1 bay leaf

1 tablespoon (9 g) peppercorns

1 tablespoon (5 g) coriander seeds

¼ cup (60 ml) dry white wine

PROCEDURE

In a large stockpot, combine all the ingredients and add enough water to cover by 2 inches (5 cm). Slowly bring the ingredients to a simmer. Simmer for 1 hour. Skim off any scum from the top that appears during cooking.

Line a colander with cheesecloth and place it over a large bowl. When the stock is done, ladle scoops of the broth through the cheesecloth to remove any impurities. Leave the bottom 1 inch (2.5 cm) of stock in the pot because it's often murky. Cool the stock and use as necessary.

Refrigerate in an airtight container for up to 5 days or freeze for up to one year.

ACKNOWLEDGMENTS

First and foremost, I need to thank everyone who bought *Venison* and, apparently, gave enough positive feedback that I've now written this second cookbook. In my wildest dreams I never thought I'd have the opportunity to write one cookbook, much less two. So thank you, from the depths of my heart; I truly appreciate it. I also need to thank all the great fishermen who showed me their secret spots and let me on their boats for a day of fishing,

ABOUT THE AUTHOR

Educated at New York City's French Culinary Institute, Jon Wipfli left behind the world of high-end commercial kitchens to form Slay to Gourmet and Animales Barbeque Co., businesses that focus on field-to-table cooking, cater private events, and serve the general public damn fine barbecue. He is the author of *Venison: The Slay to Gourmet Field to Kitchen Cookbook*. Jon lives in Minneapolis, Minnesota.

INDEX